Cheers for Coll

My son went off to University thinking he knew it all. It appears he is very hungry. Your College Cuisine could be redemption. **(B.H., Edmonton, AB)**

College Cuisine is absolutely the best little cookbook. I am ordering 8 more copies. **(E.C., Minitonas, MB)**

It's like having a mom in your kitchen. **(J.D., Swalwell, AB)**

I think your cookbook can reach a much bigger audience than the students: bachelors, freshly divorced men (...) and all people on the go, with no time to cook and on a tight budget. **(P.G., Montreal, QC)**

Please send your College Cuisine to my daughter at University. I've seen her pantry!! She definitely needs help! **(S.S., Mississauga, ON)**

Our son will be entering University next year and is determined to get away from home. Your book sounds like a perfect gift for him. **(C.L., Scarborough, ON)**

Your College Cuisine is such a fun reading book and full of delightful recipes. My husband & I (both 78 years) like to take the easy way when preparing our meals. I wouldn't part with my copy for anything. **(D.J.W., Prescott, AZ)**

Please send me ten copies. The ladies in my T'ai Chi group are back to cooking for one or two. They liked your book since most of their books are from when they were cooking for a family. Another thing they liked was the use of the kind of ingredients you are apt to have. We are all pre-gourmet and aren't interested in recipes which call for some exotic ingredient we may never use again. **(A.T.B., Lindsay, ON)**

I think your cookbook is wonderful. I have so many grand nieces and nephews of college age, I am sending for ten of them. **(I.D., Weyburn, SK)**

What a great graduation gift! **(B.M.C., Don Mills, ON)**

My grandson will be moving into his own apartment. He can cook the odd thing now but I'm sure he will need your College Cuisine cookbook to save him from malnutrition or starving to death. **(G.S., Regina, SK)**

The two granddaughters are very happy & more than satisfied. The older one has made quite an impression with your College Cuisine amongst other students and also made more friends at University. **(W.D., Carignan, QC)**

I have received the copy of College Cuisine which I ordered for my son and I like it so much I'd like a copy for myself. **(J.K., Minnedosa, MB)**

I received a similar cookbook when I first moved out, but the recipes in College Cuisine are a lot more concise and seem like real meals and not thrown together fast foods. The recipes are for actual meals rather than just throwing a sauce on pasta, and they are easy to follow. **(F.L., Red River, MB)**

Don't let students leave home without this cookbook. **(Della Radcliffe, Home Ec., Farmlife)**

College Cuisine is a basic, sensible cookbook with simple, fast and inexpensive recipes. (Peltosaari) believes that once students learn the most basic cooking skills it will serve them for life. **(Canadian Press)**

There is, indeed, life after take-out pizza. College Cuisine is a user-friendly cookbook of easy, fast, cheap and nutritious recipes. Students don't want to blow phone-bill or Thursday-night-bar money on cooking. Peltosaari recognized how thin students' wallets can be - that's what prompted her to write the book. All the recipes are economical, with some costing pennies per serving. **(Montreal Gazette)**

Making own meals saves college kids thousands of dollars. **(The Daily Courier, Kelowna, BC)**

COLLEGE CUISINE

Easy, cheap, fast, nutritious recipes for students

by Leila Peltosaari

illustrated by Julie Northey

Second edition, completely revised

Leila cooks and writes, Julie draws, and happy chaos becomes a book...

Published by: Tikka Books, PO Box 242
Chambly Quebec J3L 4B3 Canada
Tel. (450) 658-6205, FAX (450) 658-3514
web-site: www.tikkabooks.qc.ca
email: lpeltosaari@tikkabooks.qc.ca

Other books by Leila Peltosaari Albala:

Easy Sewing for Infants
Easy Sewing for Children
Easy Sewing for Adults
Easy Halloween Costumes for Children
Catalogue of Canadian Catalogues
Hey Kids... Let's Make Gifts!

Design, cover concept & icons by Albert Albala

Canadian Cataloguing in Publication Data

Peltosaari, Leila, 1947-
College cuisine: easy, cheap, fast, nutritious recipes for students

2nd completely revised ed.
Includes index.
ISBN 1-896106-01-3

1. Quick and easy cookery. 2. Low budget cookery.
1. Northey, Julie, 1956- II. Title.

TX715.6.P42 1998 641.5'5 C98-901305-7

Printed in Canada

FOREWORD

College Cuisine is definitely a basic, thrifty, sensible cookbook. Don't let them leave home without it. There is something in this book for everyone, from the college student who is learning to live on his or her own to the well-seasoned cook. It includes recipes that will lead everyone to balanced nutrition and inspired hospitality.

Read it, cook from it... be enriched in both body and spirit.

Della Radcliffe, Home Economist, Cardale, Manitoba

WITH WARMEST THANKS

For tasting and testing, recipes and ideas, humor and criticism, encouragement and support, I wish to thank my children, Albert ("Rami") and Rina, and family and friends near and far: Elie Albala, Esther Albala, Francine Boucher, Dena Bracken, Jeanine Corbin, Ellen Dick, Betty Ethier, Hugo Frappier, Barb Griffin, Helen Hartnell, Margaretha Hefti, Bernice Huxtable, Ulla Lehtonen, Owen Moran, Judy Morningstar, Lawrence and Ono Northey, Maarit Peltosaari, Benjamin Racette Lussier, Della Radcliffe, Tracy Radcliffe, Anita Reiniö, Gregory Rozee, Lydie Servanin, Elsa Trejo, A. Veller, and Cheryl Wiese. And my heartfelt thanks to Linda Bernier, Michelle Bucheck, and Susan Woodruff for proofreading, to Anneli Lukka for the photography, and to Julie Northey for the illustrations.

This one is for Rami, of course.

Icons Used In This Book

The following icons highlight some of the recipes:

Cheap

All recipes in this book are economical. These snacks and meals are especially cheap; some cost just pennies per serving.

Fast

Preparation time (prep.) is just minutes for all recipes in this book; cooking may take longer. See "Minute Meals" on pages 37-44. This icon in other categories means total time is brief.

Microwave

This icon shows what else you can do with a microwave oven besides heating leftovers. (Please see bottom of page 44.)

Breakfast

This icon spotlights recipes that are especially suitable for breakfast. Also see page 26.

Lunch

This icon spotlights recipes that are especially suitable for a lunch to go (make ahead when necessary). Also see page 27.

Vegetarian

See "Vegetarian" category on page 69. This icon in other categories draws your attention to recipes with no meat or chicken. Many students are at least part-time vegetarians.

Good For A Crowd

See "Crowd Pleasers" on page 83. This icon in other categories signals snacks, soups etc. that are practical and inexpensive to make in large quantities and popular when friends get together; just double or triple the recipe as needed.

Top Tips

Helpful hints throughout the book make your life easier. This icon also reminds you of selected not-to-miss recipes.

Contents

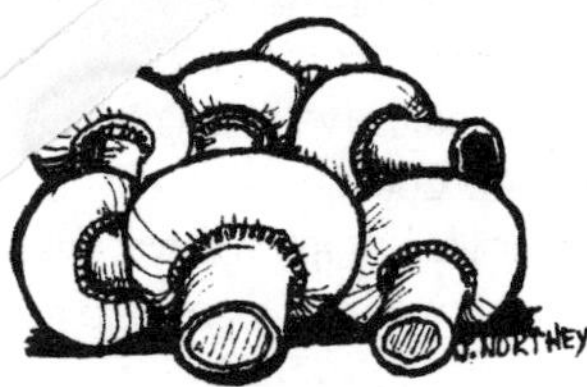

Dear Reader,

This book will bring good eating within your means, through your student years and beyond. Knowing even the most basic cooking skills will serve you for life. Once the kitchen becomes your domain, you will be able to build on your skills, experiment, and eat the results.

Eating, after all, is the most basic part of life. No matter what else is going on, you must eat something every now and then so it makes sense to learn to cook nourishing, enjoyable meals. The ritual of cooking and eating is also a great comforter, a must for life's celebrations and a soul-satisfying ritual to share with friends.

Eat with joy and enjoy your food. Don't be preoccupied with food pyramids or calorie counting and never mind about including every food group in every meal; the stress involved is not worth the trouble. Eating well is simple enough; just eat more breads and grains, pasta and rice, fruits and vegetables, beans and legumes, and drink more water; consume less fat, salt, sugar, junk food and soft drinks. But most importantly, respect your likes and dislikes. One day you might crave carrots or chocolate cake, another day junk food or heavenly soup. Your body is wise and knows best.

I have included a wide variety of recipes to make this book useful for everyone, with a specific focus on students' need for recipes that are cheap, easy, nutritious and/or fast, and made with common ingredients. The "Getting Started" category will give you handy beginner's tips on equipment, conversion tables, substitutions, and more. Do not miss the "Rescue Perishables" section; you'll turn to it whenever you wonder what to do with overripe bananas, yogurt past its prime or carrots that start growing beards. Check the comprehensive index at the back to find categories and recipes; the index includes handy check boxes to mark your favorite recipes. The icons shown on page 4 highlight some recipes that fit into more than one category and will draw your attention to recipes that are especially cheap, fast, microwavable, vegetarian, great for make-ahead breakfast/lunch, or good for a crowd.

So, clear a large area on your countertop, pick a recipe that sounds interesting and meets your time frame, line up the equipment and ingredients, and start cooking. Be a creative cook and use your imagination to alter the recipes and give them your own touch. Cooking is an adventure and a good recipe discovered is a treasure for life. I hope you will enjoy your road to culinary independence.

Getting Started

EQUIPMENT

Cooking without the proper gadgets and appliances can discourage even the most enthusiastic would-be chef. These suggestions will get you started.

ABSOLUTELY NECESSARY

DESIRABLE

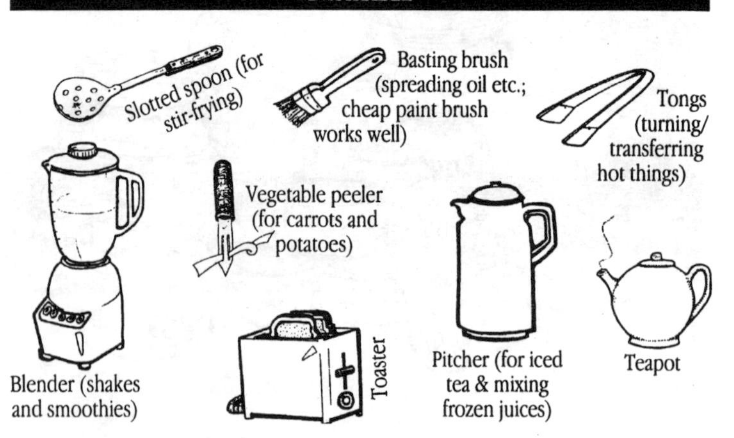

STOVETOP NECESSITIES

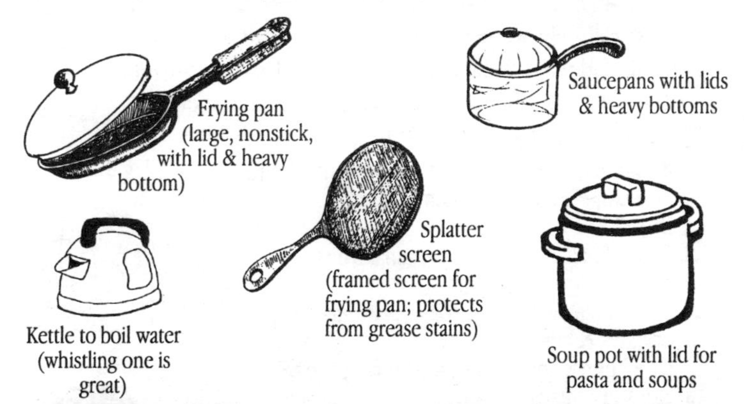

OVEN NECESSITIES

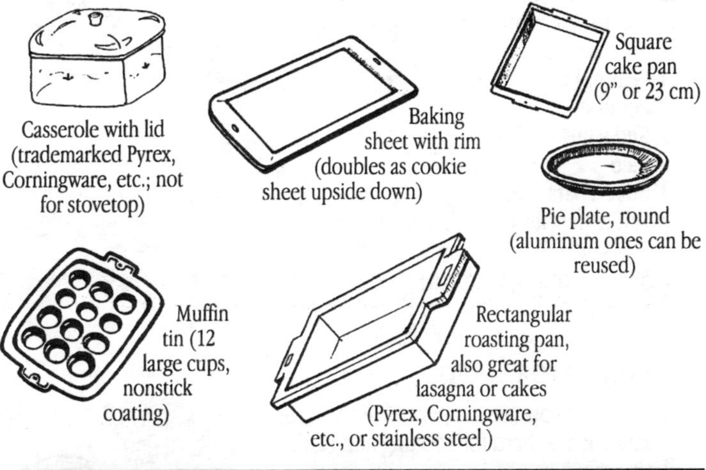

MICROWAVE NECESSITIES

- ❑ Microwavable casserole with lid
- ❑ Microwavable, shallow pie plate for frittatas (never use metal)
- ❑ Containers for portable, microwavable lunches and for heating food
- ❑ Large plastic measuring cup (handy for heating milk, making sauces)
- ❑ Pyrex glass plates, plastic plates and bowls
- ❑ Large plastic lid with vent holes to cover food. It lets the steam escape and protects the interior of your microwave. (Waxed paper or paper towels also work well.)

BASIC KITCHEN STAPLES

This list will help you get started with the most essential and common ingredients and ready-to-eat food items. You will accumulate more along the way depending on recipes and your commitment to cooking.

- ❑ All-purpose flour
- ❑ Bouillon cubes, powder, or liquid concentrate (see page 57; beef, chicken, vegetable) 
- ❑ Bread
- ❑ Cans of beans, corn, soups, tuna, fruits
- ❑ Cereals
- ❑ Coffee, tea, instant chocolate powder
- ❑ Cookies & crackers
- ❑ Dried herbs and spices (see list on page 68)
- ❑ Dry soup mixes 
- ❑ Jam
- ❑ Mustard
- ❑ Onions & garlic
- ❑ Pasta (macaroni, noodles, spaghetti) 
- ❑ Pasta sauce in jar
- ❑ Peanut butter
- ❑ Potatoes
- ❑ Red wine vinegar
- ❑ Rice
- ❑ Rolled oats
- ❑ Salt & pepper (sea salt is wonderful) 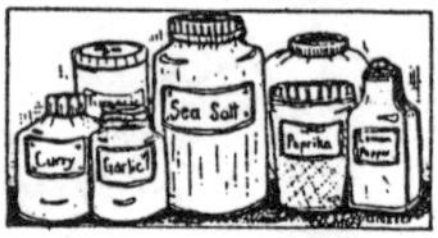
- ❑ Soy sauce (naturally brewed is best)
- ❑ Sugar (white and brown)
- ❑ Vegetable oil for cooking (canola is good); olive oil for salads (extra virgin is best)

REFRIGERATOR STAPLES

- ❑ Butter (if you use margarine, use soft for sandwiches, hard for cooking and baking)
- ❑ Cheese
- ❑ Eggs
- ❑ Flour tortillas (keep refrigerated or frozen)
- ❑ Fruits
- ❑ Lemon juice (bottled)
- ❑ Mayonnaise
- ❑ Milk
- ❑ Orange juice (or other juice)
- ❑ Plain yogurt
- ❑ Vegetables

Cooking Terms

BAKE - Cook (covered or uncovered) in an oven

BEAT - Make a mixture smooth by vigorous rotating motion using a metal whisk, fork, spoon or electric mixer.

BLEND - Combine two or more ingredients until evenly distributed.

BOIL - Heat a liquid until bubbles continuously break on the surface.

BROWN - Fry or sauté until brown.

CHOP - Cut food into small pieces with a knife.

COAT - Cover food evenly with flour, crumbs or batter.

CREAM - Make butter or other fat (at room temperature) soft and smooth by beating with a spoon, whisk or mixer.

CUBE - Cut solid food into bits of approximately the size of your fingertips.

DICE - Cut solid food into very small cubes.

DUST - Sprinkle lightly with flour, breadcrumbs or sugar.

FRY - Cook in hot frying pan or saucepan in a small amount of fat.

GRATE - Scrape or rub solid food against grater to reduce it into small particles.

GREASE - Coat or brush baking pan lightly with fat to prevent sticking (with butter or hard margarine) or spray with no-stick cooking spray.

MINCE - Cut or chop food very finely into tiny pieces.

MIX - Combine ingredients until evenly distributed.

PARBOIL - Cook food in boiling liquid until partially cooked. (Cooking is then completed by another method such as baking or roasting.)

PEEL - Cut or strip off the outer covering of fruits or vegetables.

PURÉE - Put food through a sieve, blender or processor to produce thick pulp or paste with juice.

ROAST - Cook food in an uncovered pan in the oven.

SAUTÉ - Cook or fry quickly in a small amount of fat.

SHRED - Cut food into small pieces or strips with knife/grater/shredder.

SIMMER - Cook in liquid just below the boiling point; bubbles form slowly and burst before reaching surface.

STEW - Simmer slowly in liquid deep enough to cover the food.

STIR - Mix ingredients thoroughly without beating.

STIR-FRY - Cook in a frying pan over high heat in a small amount of fat, tossing and stirring continuously with slotted spoon or spatula.

TOAST - Brown in a toaster or oven.

WHISK - Beat rapidly with a wire whisk, beater or electric mixer to incorporate air to lighten and increase volume.

Conversion Table

Imperial and metric equivalents, rounded for practical purpose.

OVEN TEMPERATURES

Fahrenheit	Celsius
275°F	140°C
300°F	150°C
325°F	160°C
350°F	175°C
375°F	190°C
400°F	200°C
425°F	220°C
450°F	230°C
475°F	240°C
500°F	260°C

SPOONS

1/4 tsp (teaspoon)	1 mL (millilitre)
1/2 tsp	2 mL
1 tsp	5 mL
1 tbsp (3 tsp)	15 mL

CAKE PANS, BAKING SHEETS, CASSEROLES & PIE PLATES

8" x 8"	20 x 20 cm
9" x 9"	23 x 23 cm
9" x 13" x 2"	23 x 33 x 5 cm
11" x 17" x 1"	28 x 43 x 2.5 cm
8-cup	2 L
10-cup	2.5 L
14-cup	3.5 L
9" x 1-1/2" (round)	23 x 4 cm
10" x 1-3/4" (round)	25 x 4.5 cm

CUPS

1/4 cup (4 tbsp)	50-60 mL
1/3 cup (5 tbsp)	75 mL
1/2 cup (8 tbsp)	125 mL
2/3 cup (10 tbsp)	160 mL
3/4 cup (12 tbsp)	180 mL
1 cup (16 tbsp)	250 mL
4 cups	1000 mL (1 L)

DRY MEASUREMENTS

1 oz.	30 g
4 oz. (1/4 lb.)	125 g
8 oz. (1/2 lb.)	250 g
16 oz. (1 lb.)	500 g
32 oz. (2 lb.)	1000 g (1 kg)

MEASURING BUTTER

1 cup = 2 sticks = 16 tbsp = 250 g = 250 mL
1/2 cup = 1 stick = 8 tbsp = 125 g = 125 mL
1/4 cup = 1/2 stick = 4 tbsp = 60 g = 60 mL

SUBSTITUTIONS

If you don't have this......	use this......
Breadcrumbs, dried	Crushed cereal or crackers
Brown sugar	White sugar (mixed with molasses if desired)
Butter	Margarine (hard, for cooking)
Buttermilk, 1 cup (250 mL)	1 cup (250 mL) milk and 1 tbsp (15 mL) lemon juice or vinegar
Buttermilk, 1 cup (250 mL)	1 cup (250 mL) plain yogurt
Cheese, old cheddar, shredded	Mild cheddar and a pinch of each of Worchestershire sauce and dry mustard
Chocolate, baking (1 oz. / 1 square) (unsweetened)	3 tbsp (45 mL) cocoa and 1 tbsp (15 mL) butter or oil
Cornstarch (1 tbsp or 15 mL)	Flour (2 tbsp or 30 mL)
Cream	Evaporated skim milk or plain yogurt
Garlic, 1-2 cloves	1/2 tsp (2 mL) dried granulated garlic (or powder; *not garlic salt*)
Herbs, fresh, 1 tbsp (15 mL)	1 tsp (5 mL) dried herbs
Honey	Sugar and liquid (water)
Lemon juice (1 tsp or 5 mL)	Vinegar (1/2 tsp or 2 mL)
Milk, 1 cup (250 mL)	1/2 cup (125 mL) evaporated milk and 1/2 cup (125 mL) water
Pizza sauce	Pasta sauce or salsa
Salsa	Pasta sauce (add herbs and spices)
Skim milk, 1 cup (250 mL)	1 cup (250 mL) water and 3 tbsp (45 mL) skim milk powder
Sour cream, 1 cup (250 mL)	1 cup (250 mL) plain yogurt (and 1-2 tsp or 5-10 mL melted butter)
Vinegar (1/2 tsp or 2 mL)	Lemon juice (1 tsp or 5 mL)
Yogurt	Milk and 1 tbsp (15 mL) lemon juice or vinegar; or buttermilk

SHOPPING

Shopping can be frustrating and time-consuming, but you can save time and money with clever planning. Look at the recipes you want to make before you go shopping; plan for portable lunches too. Stick a grocery list on the fridge and write down the ingredients whenever you think of something you need.

◆ **Get to know your local grocery store.** Shopping takes less time if you do it according to the store's layout and are able to find products fast. Shop only once a week or so and plan ahead accordingly. Lists really do work.

◆ **Bulk food sections save money.** Staples keep for weeks or months, perishables for several days. **(See the shelf life chart of perishables on pages 20-21.)** Shop for meat or chicken only when you plan to use it. While meat can be frozen, sometimes it is easier and less time-consuming to buy it fresh and use it right away. Then you don't have to remember to defrost it first. Fresh tastes better too.

◆ **The healthiest and the most economical, versatile and delicious foods are beans, pasta, rice and potatoes (see pages 30-36).** If you have them in your cupboard plus a few staples, you can always make a good meal fast for pennies. In-season fruits and vegetables are at their best and most economical. Never buy dented cans; they can be dangerous to your health. No-name or store brands are the most economical.

◆ **Buy spices and herbs in bulk without fancy packaging.** Small, plain glass jars with perforated tops are sold cheap near bulk food or in dollar stores. Better yet, save all small glass jars from jams and peanut butter for your herbs and spices. Store herbs and spices away from sunlight. Start a miniature garden on your sunny windowsill to grow herbs like parsley, mint and basil.

◆ **If you are community-minded, start a mini food co-op.** Shop at food markets and discount clubs and split those big bags with friends. And while you are at it, think about cooking together and sharing the results. Students are generally short of money but it's a lot of fun to put together great parties where everyone brings a dish or shares costs and the work load.

◆ **If you have an ethnic market nearby, discover cuisines of the world through authentic ingredients and specialties (great selections/ low prices).** Learn ethnic recipes from students of other countries. Middle-Eastern, Mediterranean, Oriental and Latin-American cuisines and others from all corners of the world bring you many exciting culinary alternatives.

MISTAKES

Mistakes are your best teachers, but should you eat them? Throwing them out is a waste of money and you are hungry anyway so rescue them if you can.

◆ **Overcooked vegetables.** Do not drain. Make a chowder by adding a little extra water, interesting herbs/spices and some milk (see page 56 for a recipe). Or purée the overcooked veggies and use them for a soup or sauce; add a splash of milk, grated cheese etc. depending on the situation.

◆ **Burned food?** Do not stir. Immediately transfer the unburned portion to a clean saucepan (then scrape out and discard the burned portion), check the taste to see if it's edible and if so, add some spices or liquid.

◆ **Food is always burning?** Get quality pots with heavy bottoms. Your pots and frying pans are probably not thick enough.

◆ **Soggy rice?** Do not stir. Open the lid slightly so the water can evaporate, and cook a little longer.

◆ **Raw rice?** Add a bit of water, stir, cover tightly and cook a little longer.

◆ **Food won't brown?** Your oven is too cool or the food has too much liquid. Pour off excess liquid and/or slightly raise the oven temperature.

◆ **Too salty or too spicy?** Make some more pasta, potatoes, rice, beans or whatever you are making without using salt or spices, then mix together with the salty/spicy food. Salty soup? Remove some of the salty liquid, replace with water. Or add 2-3 potatoes, peeled & cut into chunks. Cook until tender, then remove and discard the potatoes which will have absorbed excess salt.

◆ **Soup is too thin?** Add a boiled or microwaved mashed potato, or add a bit of flour or cornstarch mixed with cold water.

◆ **Overcooked in oven, too dry?** Add butter, oil, water or plain yogurt, whatever is appropriate, and briefly cook on stovetop to blend the flavors.

◆ **Something went wrong and the food is bland and boring?** Rescue it with a splash of bouillon liquid concentrate or soy sauce and sprinkle with herb mix. Season lightly since adding is always easier than removing.

◆ **Overcooked pasta?** Drain well (chop fettuccine/spaghetti), stir-fry in a bit of oil over medium high heat to crispen the mushy pasta, then add herbs, spices, soy sauce. Or make an easy and delicious pasta frittata (page 43).

SAFETY TIPS

Cooking can be dangerous so remember these basic rules in the kitchen.

• **Do not, under any circumstances, add cold water to hot oil or other hot grease.** (It will explode.) If you have a grease fire, never throw water on it. If the fire is in a pot or frying pan, cover it immediately with a lid; if it's outside the pot, throw baking soda or salt on it. Keep a small fire extinguisher around; it could save your kitchen if a fire gets out of control. Unplug, if possible, electric appliances such as kettles, toasters, coffee makers, and hair dryers, when not in use. (They might start a fire.)

• **Roll up long, loose sleeves or wear short sleeves when near a stove.** Long sleeves get in your way and can catch fire. Turn pot and frying pan handles out of your way so you won't accidentally tip them over.

• **Avoid electrocution; never immerse electric appliances in water.** Do not poke into a toaster with metal forks etc. if your toast is stuck. Unplug it first or use wooden or plastic tongs.

• **Sniff and look at everything**: raw chicken, cold cuts, canned food, leftovers, fruit, dairy products. You'll learn fast how fresh food smells and looks and will know when something is rotten. If in doubt, throw it out. Check best-before-dates on packages when shopping; often the fresher ones are kept at the back to move out the older stuff first. **Uncooked meat may be safely refrigerated for up to four days, ground meat and raw fish for up to two days.** Leave meat and chicken in the store wrap and refrigerate until used since repeated handling can spread bacteria in the food and around your kitchen. Once cooked, meat keeps for several days. Make it a practice to cook and eat any meat as soon as possible; it's safer and it tastes, smells and looks better. If you cannot use ground meat by the second day, brown it and refrigerate for another day or two, then use it in a recipe. Or freeze it, raw or cooked. Buy frozen fish and defrost only when needed (overnight in your refrigerator or plunged into cold water for quick defrosting). If not eaten within a day or two, freeze leftovers while they are still edible. **To avoid contamination and bacterial buildup, never refreeze defrosted raw meat without cooking it first.**

• **Kill salmonella and E.coli bacteria.** Handle raw poultry and meat separately from any other food. Thoroughly wash utensils, boards and hands with hot, soapy water. Never put cooked food on the same plate used for raw meat or poultry. Cook chicken/meat until it is well done. Cover and refrigerate leftovers right away, especially those containing milk or other animal products.

• **Avoid cross-contamination.** Wash your hands before cooking. Wash fruit and vegetables you are going to eat raw. Wash dishrag well after each use and hang it flat to dry over tap (or spread flat over clean countertop). Clean and refreshen it in diluted bleach or toss it in a dishwasher or laundry.

• **Avoid bacterial buildup and food poisoning by washing your can opener after each use with soap and hot water.** Even electric model or wall-mounted ones must have blades cleaned after each use. Wash can tops before using a can opener. Transfer any leftovers of canned food to a glass or plastic container, cover, and refrigerate.

CLEANING

Nobody likes cleaning but you can simplify your life with clever planning.

• **Make it easy.** Use hot, soapy water to soak dirty dishes, wash and rinse.

• **Keep a folded towel in your refrigerator drawer under the vegetables to absorb the moisture. This makes cleaning easier too.**

• **Avoid doing dishes.** Peel potatoes etc. over pages of junk mail and then just wrap and toss the discards. Often you can cut chunks of onions, zucchini or tomatoes directly into the bowl or pot without using a cutting board. Add **very hot water** to your frying pan immediately after use while the pan is still hot; that's usually enough for a simple rinsing to clean it. (Exception: If you have very hot oil in the frying pan or pot, do not add water; let the oil cool first, then soak and wash the pan.) Use fewer dishes and utensils while preparing food so there will be less to wash. Reuse pans, knives, and plates for preparing different ingredients with just a rinse in between. The only exception is raw chicken or meat. Never use any dish or utensil that has touched raw chicken or meat for anything else, without washing it first in hot soapy water. Flip the chopping board over for a clean surface when needed. **Burnt food in pots and frying pans?** Remove as much as possible with spoon or spatula, fill pan with water and bring to a boil, remove from heat, Add a bit of baking soda or a squirt of dishwashing liquid, let cool and use a spatula to loosen what you can, then scrub well.

• **Recycle whenever possible.** Reuse strong plastic containers and glass jars with lids for refrigerating, freezing and microwaving leftover foods. Use the biggest ones for storing dried beans, rice, flour and sugar. Reuse aluminum pie plates and strong freezer bags several times. The smallest containers with lids are perfect for herbs and spices and for salad dressings (page 50).

• **Don't leave road maps for ants and other little bugs.** Clean off sticky threads of molasses, syrup, oil, jam, ketchup, honey etc. from bottles and jars right after use. This also makes them easier to use next time.

• **Avoid unnecessary mess when greasing.** Using nonstick cooking spray makes for quick and easy clean-up. Or line baking sheets and pans with parchment paper, waxed paper or foil depending on the situation. Use a nonstick frying pan and baking sheet for fast cleaning. Line muffin tins with paper cups. If you must grease, keep your hand clean by slipping it inside a plastic bag to spread the grease on cookie sheets and in casseroles.

• **Cover all leftovers and refrigerate.** Do not forget to eat them while they are still edible. Or freeze them as soon as possible in containers or freezer-strength plastic bags; add a date & label so you won't wonder later what it is.

• **Clean essential cooking equipment after each use.** Clean and rinse as you go whenever possible to prevent dirty dishes from accumulating and food from drying. Always wash the grater right after each use with a brush so cheese or garlic won't dry on the inner surface. For easy cleaning and to eliminate an unpleasant odor, first rinse with cold water all dishes that have been used to prepare, cook or serve eggs, then wash in hot soapy water. A plastic dishpan frees up the sink and is handy to stack, carry and soak the dirty dishes.

• **Clean spilled food in oven or on stovetop immediately. If not cleaned right away, it only gets worse when reheated.** For easy cleaning, sprinkle spills in your oven immediately with salt, remove what you can with a metal spatula as soon as the oven has cooled off, then clean with a wet plastic scrubber and dishrag. Use big enough saucepans and casseroles so food won't spill over in the first place. Put a baking sheet or aluminum foil under the casserole (or line oven floor with foil) to catch spills if the casserole is so full that it might spill over.

• **Avoid stains. An inexpensive splatter guard for your frying pan prevents greasy stains on your clothes and stovetop.** Don't wear your best clothes thinking that you'll be careful; use an apron or at least wrap a kitchen towel around your waist to protect clothing. OK, you messed up and wonder how to get rid of that greasy stain. Saturate the grease stain immediately with dishwashing liquid to cut the grease (this works well on many other stains, too), then launder in hot water with detergent.

RESCUE

SHELF LIFE OF PERISHABLES

Food item	Refrigerator (40°F or 4°C)	Freezer (0°F or -18°C)
Apples (February-July)	2 weeks	1 year
Apples (August-January)	6 months	1 year
Beans and lentils, cooked	5 days	3 months
Beef (steaks, roast)	3-5 days	6-12 months
Blueberries	5 days	1 year
Butter, salted*	3 weeks	1 year
Butter, unsalted*	3 weeks	3 months
Carrots	3 months	1 year
Casseroles	2-3 days	3 months
Celery	2 weeks	•
Cheese, hard, cheddar etc.	5 weeks	6 months
Cheese, blue*	1 week	•
Cheese, Camembert, Brie	3-4 weeks	•
Cheese, cottage, Ricotta*	3-5 days	•
Cheese, cream cheese*	2-3 weeks	•
Chicken, cooked, with sauce	1-2 days	6 months
Chicken, cooked, without sauce	3-4 days	1-3 months
Chicken, fresh, pieces	1-2 days	6-9 months
Chicken, fresh, whole	1-3 days	10-12 months
Cold cuts (ham, turkey), cooked*	3-4 days	1-2 months
Cold cuts (ham, turkey), smoked*	5-6 days	1-2 months
Eggs, hardcooked, in shell	1 week	•
Eggs, raw, in shell	1 month	•
Egg yolk, raw	2-3 days	4 months
Egg white, raw	1 week	9 months
Fish, fresh, fat	1-2 days	2 months
Fish, fresh, slim	2-3 days	6 months
Fish, cold-smoked	3-4 days	2 months
Fresh herbs	4 days	1 year
Fruit & vegetable juices*	1-2 weeks	1 year
Ham, cooked, whole	7 days	1-2 months
Ice cream	•	3 months
Ketchup & bottled sauces*	1 year	•
Lettuce, cucumber	1 week	•
Margarine*	1 month	3 months
Mayonnaise*	2 months	•
Meat, cooked, with sauce	3-4 days	4 months
Meat, cooked, without sauce	3-4 days	2-3 months
Meat, minced or cubed, raw	1-2 days	3-4 months
Meat sauces	3-5 days	4-6 months
Milk*	3-5 days	6 weeks
Mushrooms	5 days	1 year
Mustard, prepared	1 year	•
Nuts	4-6 months	1 year
Pastry (with milk & eggs)	3-4 days	1 month
Pasta, cooked	3-5 days	3 months
Pâté, meat	2-3 days	3 months
Pork (chops etc.)	3-5 days	4-6 months
Rice, cooked	5-6 days	6-8 months
Rice, brown, uncooked	6-9 months	•
Sandwiches	1-2 days	6 weeks
Sausages, dry, whole	2-3 weeks	•
Sausages, fresh	1-2 days	2-3 months
Soups	3 days	2-3 months
Sour cream*	3-5 days	1 month
Sprouts	3 days	•
Strawberries, raspberries	3-4 days	1 year
Tofu	1-2 weeks	1-2 months
Veal, roasted	3-5 days	4 months
Vegetables	5-7 days	•
Yogurt	2-3 weeks	1 month
Watermelon, honeydew, cantaloupe	4 days	•
Whole-wheat flour	3 months	6-9 months

***After opening; also check best-before dates.**

Products With Longer Shelf Life

Food item	Room temperature
Baking chocolate	7 months
Baking powder	1 year
Baking soda	1 year
Beans & lentils, dried	1 year
Breadcrumbs, dry	3 month
Breads (in plastic bag, sliced)	1 week
Bread, fresh, baguette	1-2 days
Cake mixes	1 year
Cereals	6-8 months
Cocoa powder	10-12 months
Coffee, freshly ground*	1 month
Coffee, instant	1 year
Coffee whitener (cream substitute)	6 months
Cookies & crackers	6 months
Dried fruits	1 year
Dry mustard powder	3 years
Evaporated canned milk, unsweetened	9-12 months
Evaporated canned milk, sweetened	6 months
Flour, all-purpose	2 years
Herbs and spices, dried	1 year
Honey	18 months
Jams and jellies	1 year
Jelly powder	2 years
Maple syrup, corn syrup	1 year
Molasses	2 years
Nuts	1 month
Olives	1 year
Onions, at room temperature	1 day
Onions, in cold room	3-4 weeks
Olive oil (in cool, dark, do not refrigerate)*	1 year
Pasta, dry (spaghetti, fettuccine etc.)	1 year
Pasta, egg noodles	6 months
Peanut butter*	2 months
Potatoes, at room temperature	1 week
Potatoes, in cold room	9 months
Preserves	1 year
Pudding mixes	18 months
Rice, white	1 year
Rolled oats	6-10 months
Sugar	2 years
Skim milk powder*	1 month
Syrup	1 year
Tea	6 months
Vegetable oil	1 year
Vinegar	2 years

***After opening; also check best-before dates.**

(This is a partial list provided by Government of Quebec, Ministry of Agriculture. For updates and more information, please visit the College Cuisine web-site at: www.tikkabooks.qc.ca.)

RESCUE PERISHABLES

Practical Tips

After their recommended shelf life, most food products can still be safely used but their taste and nutrition value may have deteriorated. All canned goods, after opening, must be transferred to glass or plastic containers and refrigerated. Dry cereals should be stored in sealed containers away from heat and light. Ideally, frozen food should be defrosted in the refrigerator; use a plate underneath so the liquids won't drip over other food items. To prevent contamination and bacterial buildup, never refreeze raw meat that has been defrosted; cook it first if you must refreeze it. Partially cook vegetables before freezing. Use only freezer bags specifically meant for food products. Add a label to indicate content and date. Periodically check the temperature; your refrigerator should be 40°F (4°C) or less; your freezer should be 0°F (-18°C).

Recipes For Perishables

It's good to come home to delicious leftovers. Even if you only cook for one or two and the recipe serves four or more, make the whole batch so tomorrow's cooking is easy and requires just heating. Divide extra food, including plain rice and beans, into small portions for one or two and freeze in strong, self-sealing freezer-strength/microwavable plastic bags (they can be reused repeatedly). Then toss a bag into your microwave (or empty its contents into a saucepan to heat) whenever needed.

What to do with leftovers and other perishables before it's too late? Lots of things, including the following (page number shown in brackets after recipe):

- **Apples**: Apple delight (111), Apple oatmeal crisp for two (115)
- **Avocado:** Freezing (96), Gourmet melt (42), Guacamole (96)
- **Bagels:** Bagel bits (95), Gourmet melt (42)
- **Baguette:** Baguette bits (95), Baguette cinnamon crisps (110)
- **Bananas:** Banana Muffins (101), Fried bananas (114), Frozen bananas (114), Milkshakes & smoothies (117), Sweet snacks (110)
- **Bean sprouts:** Chicken chop suey (62)
- **Beans, cooked or canned:** Bean burritos (39), Bean spread (39), Bean tofu burgers (73), Beans & rice (39), Fried beans (40), Mexican melts (40), Minestrone soup (55), Quick quesadillas (41), Stuffed mini-pitas (84), Tacos (88), Tropical beans (81), Vegetarian chili (90)
- **Beef (cubed stewing beef, raw):** Navy bean stew (63)
- **Blue cheese:** Dips (95-96), Salad dressings (50), Stuffed mini-pitas (84)
- **Bread:** Baguette cinnamon crisps (110), Croutons (58), Dried bread (95), French toast (111), Garlic bread (95), Grilled cheese sandwich (44), French onion soup (54)
- **Broccoli:** Broccoli cheese squares (88), Broccoli potatoes (77), Chinese chicken and vegetables (89), Creamy pasta veggie combo (78), Vegetable chowder (56)
- **Buttermilk**: Oat flatbread (104), Salad dressings (50)
- **Cabbage:** Coleslaw for crowd (47), Colorful coleslaw for one (46)
- **Carrots:** Carrot pineapple muffins (99), Chinese chicken and vegetables (89), Chicken chop suey (62), Colorful coleslaw for one (46), Creamy pasta veggie combo (78), Glazed carrots (75), Italian spaghetti sauce (85), Kielbasa casserole (64), Roasted vegetables (75), Soups and chowders (51-58), Sunshine salad (46), Tofu risotto (78), Zucchini fritters or frittata (82)
- **Celery:** Chicken chop suey (62), Chinese chicken and vegetables (89), Chinese fried rice (72), Italian spaghetti sauce (85), Pasta salad (48), Roasted vegetables (75), Soups & chowders (51-58), Tofu risotto (78), Tuna salad (49)
- **Chicken, cooked:** Curry chicken (60). Or make a soup: Chicken leftovers, chopped vegetables, water, bouillon cube, noodles; simmer until tender.
- **Chicken, raw:** Baked chicken (60), Chicken chop suey (62), Chicken soup (58), Chinese chicken (89), Roasted drumsticks (62), Senegalese peanut sauce & chicken (68)

- **Cottage cheese:** Broccoli cheese squares (88), Spinach mini-quiches (90), Sweet snacks (110), Vegetarian lasagna (93)
- **Cream:** Russian quiche (91), Salad dressings (50)
- **Cream cheese:** Broccoli potatoes (77), Cheese soup (53), Chocolate cheesecake (103), Dips (96), Salad dressings (50), Sweet snacks (110)
- **Eggs, hard-boiled:** Bean spread (39), Egg butter (104), Egg dip (96), Egg salad sandwich (28), Stuffed mini-pitas (84). Or, make Béchamel sauce (92), add crushed, hard-boiled eggs, and eat with cooked potatoes.
- **Feta cheese:** Feta dip (96), Greek salad (49), Spinach mini-quiches (90), Stuffed mini-pitas (84)
- **Fish (uncooked):** Baked fish and vegetables (61), Crunchy baked fish fillets (65), Seafood chowder (57)
- **Flour tortillas:** Bean burritos (39), Tortilla chips (95), Tortilla pizzas (38)
- **French fries (fresh or frozen):** Poutine (92)
- **Fruit juices:** Smoothies (117)
- **Fruit:** Fruit salad (110), Shakes and smoothies (117). Grapes, watermelon & other fruit can be frozen into delicious treats (114).
- **Garlic:** Grate garlic cloves, freeze in thin layer in plastic bag, break off a piece as needed. Freeze whole garlic cloves, unpeeled; peel & grate frozen cloves as needed.
- **Gingerroot (fresh):** Chinese chicken and vegetables (89), Chinese fried rice (72), Orange ginger sauce (112), Senegalese peanut sauce & chicken (68), Tofu risotto (78), Tropical beans (81). Freezing fresh gingerroot: See page 57.
- **Ground beef:** Chili con carne (87), Hamburgers (66), Italian spaghetti sauce (85), Meat and macaroni casserole (67), Meatballs (86), Stovetop rice and meat (63), Stuffed mini-pitas (84), Tacos (88)
- **Ham (cooked or smoked):** Caribbean rice & ham (64), Pasta frittata (43), Pizza (94), Russian quiche (91)
- **Leek:** Baked fish and vegetables (61), Leek and potato soup (53)
- **Lemons:** To make them extra-juicy (and for long storage), cut lemons in half and freeze in a small plastic bag; defrost in microwave and squeeze as needed. Chinese chicken and vegetables (89), Crunchy baked fish fillets (65), Eat-them-like-fries (44), Glazed carrots (75), Hummus (79), Salad dressings (50), Salads (46-49)
- **Meat, cooked:** Pasta frittata (43). **Raw meat:** See beef or ground beef.
- **Milk:** Baked fish and vegetables (61), Béchamel sauce (92), Café au lait (116), Cheese biscuits (98), Cheese soup (53), Cream of mushroom soup (55), Creamy pasta veggie combo (78), Creamy potato soup for two (52), Crêpes (112), Cupcakes (105), French toast (111), Kielbasa casserole (64), Macaroni and cheese casserole (76), Mashed potatoes (70), Meat and macaroni casserole (67), Milkshakes (117), Pancakes & baked pancake (113), Pasta frittata (43), Quick pop-up rolls (104), Seafood chowder (57), Vegetable chowder (56)
- **Mushrooms, fresh:** Cheese soup (53), Cream of mushroom soup (55), Crêpes (112), French onion soup (54), Omelet (31), Chunky pasta sauce (40), Pizza (94), Roasted vegetables (75), Stuffed mini-pitas (84), Tofu risotto (78), Vegetarian lasagna (93)

- **Parsley, fresh:** Bean spread (39), Couscous salad (48), Tofu risotto (78)
- **Pasta, cooked:** Baked ziti (74), Creamy corn casserole (74), Macaroni and cheese casserole (76), Pasta frittata (43), Pasta salad (48).
- **Pasta sauce:** Baked ziti (74), Bean burritos (39), Chunky pasta sauce (40), Hot Russian sandwich (41), Humble rice bake (44), Stuffed mini-pitas (84), Tortilla pizzas (38), Vegetarian lasagna (93).
- **Pineapple (canned):** Carrot pineapple muffins (99), Bean burritos (39), Fried bananas (114), Frozen sweet stuff (114), Sweet snacks (110), Shakes and smoothies (117), Tropical beans (81)
- **Pita:** Chips (95-96), Pita melts (42), Sandwiches (28)
- **Potatoes (cooked or baked):** Quick potato salad (46). Cold, cooked potatoes are tasty as is. Or fry some in butter, add salt and pepper.
- **Potatoes (raw):** Baked potato skins (71), Broccoli potatoes (77), Creamy potato soup for two (52), Kielbasa casserole (64), Leek and potato soup (53), Mashed potatoes & potato patties (70), Potato frittata (77), Roasted vegetables (75), Scalloped potatoes for one (41), Soups and chowders (51-58)
- **Raisins:** Banana muffins (101), Bran oat muffins (102), Crunchy granola cakes (98), Chewy oatmeal cookies (108), Sweet snacks (110)
- **Rice, cooked:** Bean tofu burgers (73), Chinese fried rice (72), Curry chicken (60), Humble rice bake (44), Rice salad (46), Stuffed mini-pitas (84), Tropical beans (81)
- **Ricotta cheese:** Feta dip (96), Stuffed mini-pitas (84)
- **Salsa:** Bean burritos (39), Rich nachos (38)
- **Sausage:** Kielbasa casserole (64), Pasta frittata (43), Poutine (92)
- **Skim milk powder:** Cuban crush (117). Use also in casseroles, baking, chowders and other recipes requiring milk (see milk on page 23).
- **Sour cream:** Cheese biscuits (98), Chocolate cheesecake (103), Dips (95-96), Salad dressings (50), Tzatziki (96)
- **Spinach (fresh or frozen):** Pizza (94), Russian quiche (91), Spinach mini-quiches (90), Stuffed mini-pitas (84), Vegetarian lasagna (93)
- **Tofu (see page 81):** Bean tofu burgers (73), Tofu fricassée (79), Tofu risotto (78), Tofu sandwich (76), Tofu, veggies & couscous (89)
- **Tomato paste (purée):** Spoon leftovers from can into plastic freezer bag, close & press flat into a thin layer, freeze, then break off a piece when needed.
- **Vegetables (raw or cooked):** Cheese soup (53), Chinese chicken and vegetables (89), Chinese fried rice (72), Chunky pasta sauce (40), Minestrone soup (55), Ratatouille (80), Roasted vegetables (75), Stuffed mini-pitas (84), Tacos (88), Tofu, veggies & couscous (89), Vegetable chowder (56), Vegetarian lasagna (93)
- **Whole-wheat flour:** Muffins (99-102)
- **Yogurt (plain):** Blueberry muffins (100), Salad dressings (50), Sweet snacks (110), Tropical thick shake (117), Tzatziki (96)
- **Zucchini:** Baked fish and vegetables (61), Chinese fried rice (72), Curry chicken (60), Ratatouille (80), Roasted vegetables (75), Zucchini sauté (42), Zucchini fritters (82), Zucchini sticks (73)

Breakfasts, Lunches To Go, Sandwiches

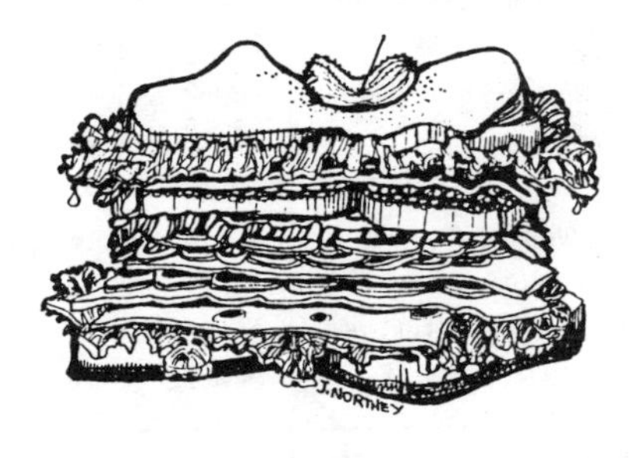

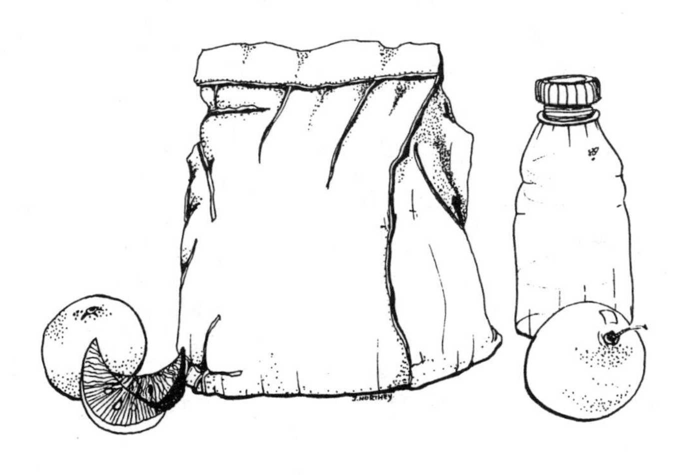

Breakfasts

Sleep is so sweet in the morning that you may prefer another snooze to breakfast, but if you rush out without any food, you'll get very hungry and tire soon. At least drink something, even just water which actually is the best thing around. Some people prefer sweet stuff in the morning, others crave salty things. Any food can be breakfast.

Keep some orange juice, iced tea (116), cold water, milk, in your refrigerator for replenishing fluids. It takes just seconds to quench your thirst.	Fruit is good and fast in the morning, portable and eatable anywhere (bananas, apples, grapes, mandarins etc.). Yogurt with fruit & granola takes just minutes.
Split, toasted bagel with cream cheese is divine. You'll never outgrow toast with peanut butter and jam. Make a sandwich to go the night before (see page 28).	See sweet snacks (page 110). If you have ten minutes, make Melba Melts (page 43) or Pita Melts (42), café au lait (116) or hot chocolate in the microwave.
Cold leftovers, anything goes. Pizza, ham, chicken, pancakes, meatballs, beans, potato, pasta, hard-boiled egg, sausages, indeed anything... Save something from supper the night before.	Cereals without milk (Granola, Spoon-Size Shredded Wheat, Cheerios, Rice Krispies etc.) in self-sealing plastic bag (to eat on the run) is not bad at all if you have something to drink on the side.
Make muffins (99-102), cookies (107-108), crunchy granola cakes (98), oat flatbread (104), pancakes (113) in advance for a delicious breakfast. You can eat them on the run.	Make scrambled eggs or an omelet (page 31). Throw in leftover rice, pasta, beans or potatoes, grated cheese. Add toast & a glass of orange juice or hot tea and you'll survive for many hours.
Heavenly treat for a lazy morning: Quick smoothie (117), and French Toast with hot Apple Delight (recipes are on page 111), topped with vanilla ice cream.	Don't forget good old-fashioned hot oatmeal and cream of wheat; the recipes are on the boxes. They are nourishing and soul-satisfying.
Bagel bits from wholegrain bagels with raisins (page 95) and baguette cinnamon crisps (page 110) are easy to make, taste delicious and can be dipped into your hot drink.	Lots of time for a civilized sit-down breakfast/brunch? Make Crêpes, Baked Pancake or eggs. Brew a pot of coffee or tea. A tray of fruit, bread/bagels, butter, cheese, jam, cucumber and tomatoes.

Lunches To Go

Reserve time in your weekly schedule to make food for lunches. A couple of hours a week of planning and preparing can eliminate the stress related to making lunch every day. If you must eat on the go, think ahead and prepare something portable. If you usually oversleep, prepare your lunch the night before so you can just grab the bag on your way out.

For perishable food, use an insulated vacuum container which works for both hot and cold food. A lunch box with a frozen ice pack keeps things cold too. (Mayonnaise-laced food must not be kept at room temperature for a long time, especially in hot weather and when mixed with any animal products. Mayonnaise is available in small individual serving-size packets which you can open and mix with the rest when it's time to eat.)

Most important is to satisfy thirst. Carry a bottle of water in your backpack, refill at water coolers. Much better than soft drinks, it satisfies thirst best, the price is right and you can take a swig anywhere.	Perfect for a cold lunch: Sesame oat veggie burgers (72), bean tofu burgers (73), spinach mini-quiches (90), frittatas (pasta, 43, potato, 77, zucchini, 82), meatballs (86), pasta salad (48).
Fruit is always a perfect and satisfying snack: apples, grapes, bananas and mandarins etc. Slit orange peel partially with knife to get a good start and peel the rest with your fingers when ready.	Carrot and celery sticks in self-sealing bag are good for lunch. Dates, prunes, raisins etc., peanuts, roasted sunflower seeds and pumpkin seeds make great snacks anytime, anywhere.
A pita makes a perfect sandwich and becomes an edible, spillproof pocket for whatever you stuff into it. See sandwich ideas on page 28.	Muffins, cookies, date squares, crunchy granola cakes (pages 98-108), oat flatbread (page 104) make nutritious, filling, portable lunches.
If you have access to a microwave, take a container of leftovers: Minestrone soup (page 55), lentil soup (56), navy bean stew (63), tropical beans (81), chili con carne (87), bean burritos (39), ziti (74).	Make leftover macaroni or fusilli into a cold salad with chopped tomatoes, celery, hard-boiled eggs, cucumbers, a splash of salad dressing & dried herbs.

Save containers with tight lids or buy a few microwavable storage containers — they are not expensive and can be used forever. Fill with yesterday's leftovers, pasta, rice, potato, beans, cooked vegetables, plus add a few slices of tomato, perhaps some pasta sauce plus shredded cheese. Sprinkle with some herbs and spices. Heat in a microwave oven.

Sandwiches

Discover a whole world of breads! • Light European-style rye and black Russian rye breads. • Whole-wheat/multigrain. • Egg bread. • French baguette (a long, narrow loaf of French bread, also whole-wheat). • Sourdough, pumpernickel, buns and rolls. • English muffins. • Flour tortillas (many varieties). • Pita. • Bagels (sesame, black, multigrain with raisins, whole-wheat) are popular, portable, versatile, great for breakfast, lunch, snacks, everything. See "Minute Meals" for hot sandwiches. Multigrain breads satisfy hunger and taste fresh for much longer than white sliced bread. Use up stale bread so you'll never waste any and will always have some around: Remove the plastic bag before bread gets moldy; dry slices at room temperature (or in the oven, low heat). Store dried slices in a covered container, dip in hot drinks & soups, or cover with cheese and bake until cheese melts. See page 22 for more ideas.

SANDWICHES

North America's favorites: Ham-and-cheese (sliced bread, mayo or mustard, some lettuce, cheese, cold cuts). Good old peanut butter & jam on toast.

Great sandwich spreads:
- Hummus (page 79)
- Guacamole (page 96)
- Cream cheese (on bagels/muffins)

Submarine: Split long bun in two. Mustard/mayo & toppings (lettuce, sautéed mushrooms & onions, tomato, pepperoni, ham, mozzarella cheese).

Great sandwich fillers: Veggie burgers (72-73), zucchini fritters (82), potato frittata (77). Tofu sandwich (76) with mustard, lettuce, sliced tomato.

Egg salad sandwich: Crush hard-boiled eggs, mix with a little mayonnaise or butter, season with salt and pepper. Use as a sandwich filler.

Hot cheese sandwich: Cover bread slice with cheese, bake for 10 minutes. **Rich version:** Under the cheese, add mustard, ham, tomato, sprinkle dried garlic on top.

Fill pita pocket with: • Shredded lettuce, leftovers (meat, chicken, vegetables, meatballs), mayonnaise or mustard. • Fresh spinach leaves, hard-boiled sliced egg, canned chickpeas, sliced tomato and cucumber, shredded carrot, plain yogurt, and simulated bacon bits. • Canned tuna or salmon, celery, onions, tomato, mayonnaise. • Canned beans, lettuce, cheese, stuffed olives, tomato, salsa or salad dressing.

Scandinavian open-faced sandwiches: Use a variety of fresh sliced bread; do not toast and do not cover your creations with another slice. Spread slices gently with soft butter, mayonnaise, cream cheese or mustard. Create different taste and color sensations with a few toppings (such as crisp spinach or lettuce, cold cuts, smoked salmon, cooked shrimp, tuna, cheese, sliced or crushed hard-boiled egg, sardines, anchovies, sliced tomato or cucumber). Use sliced, stuffed olives, chives, parsley, dill, sprouts, radish slices, red pepper strips, capers, etc. for decoration. Make a large party platter to delight your friends and collect compliments.

BASICS

SEEDS
DNEY BEANS
CKED WHEAT
OATS
ODLES
ARONI
FLOUR
RAISINS
Honey
Onions
Potato

Soft-Boiled Eggs

In small saucepan, bring to full boil enough water to cover eggs completely. With tablespoon, gently lower eggs into boiling water. Without lid, cook for exactly 5 minutes over high heat. Crack one end open and eat hot eggs with a spoon.

Hard-Boiled Eggs

Put eggs into saucepan and cover with cold water. Without lid, bring water to full boil over high heat. Remove the saucepan from heat, cover and let the eggs sit in the hot water for 15-20 minutes. Then run cold water into the saucepan to stop the cooking process and make peeling easier. Crack the peel, massage the egg between your fingertips and pull the peel off. Peeling is very easy if the egg is still warm.

Hard-boiled eggs in their shells keep several days refrigerated. Dent shells a bit (or mark with pencil) to tell them apart from raw eggs, or test by spinning on tabletop; the boiled ones spin fast. Hard-boiled eggs are tasty hot or cold, sliced on toast, or seasoned with salt and pepper. More ideas on page 23.

Fried Eggs

Sunny-side up: Melt a little butter in frying pan over high heat until sizzling. Break the egg into the hot frying pan so that the yolk remains whole. Immediately reduce the heat to medium high. Gently poke spatula tip into liquid egg white, pulling it away from around the yolk (but without breaking the yolk) so it runs underneath and cooks faster before edges become too dry. Cook until white loses transparency and is just set, about a minute or so. Lightly season with salt and pepper (and perhaps some Tabasco).

Over easy: Proceed as above but after frying one side, flip the egg over with spatula, then immediately turn heat off. Let the egg sit in the hot frying pan for a few seconds to fry it very briefly underneath.

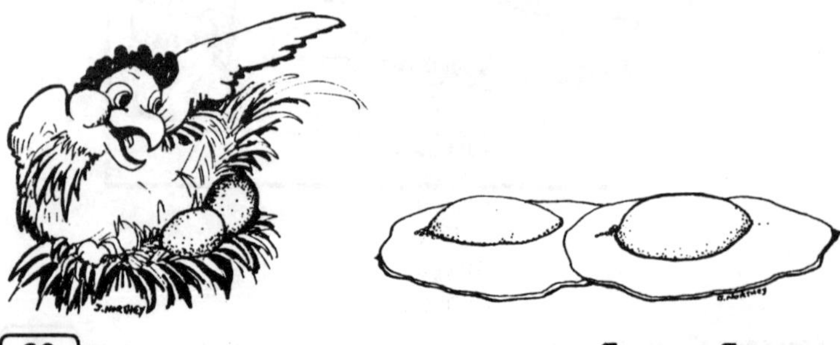

Scrambled Eggs For One

Break two eggs into a small bowl, stir with a fork to break yolks but do not mix thoroughly. Heat a little butter in nonstick frying pan over high heat for one minute until sizzling. Pour the egg mixture in the hot pan and reduce the heat to medium high. Cook for about 1-2 minutes, stirring with spatula and keeping the eggs in constant motion, until just set. Do not overcook. Season with salt and pepper. (**Variation:** Mix some grated cheese and/or cooked, chopped ham with eggs before cooking, sprinkle with herbs. Remember to stir constantly while cooking.)

Microwaved Scrambled Eggs

Break two eggs into a plastic bowl, add a teaspoonful of butter and two tablespoons of milk. Stir briefly to break egg yolks. Cover and microwave at 100% (full power) for 2 minutes. Let stand for a minute and stir. Season lightly with salt and pepper. Spread onto hot toast. (Never microwave eggs in shells since they will explode.)

Omelet For One

In small bowl or measuring cup, beat two eggs and two tablespoons of water with fork. Heat a little butter in nonstick frying pan over high heat for one minute until sizzling, tilt the pan quickly to coat the bottom and sides. Pour the egg mixture into the hot pan. Immediately reduce the heat to medium high, and stir with spatula or fork for a few seconds until eggs just start to set. Spoon shredded cheese or other fillings (mushrooms, shredded ham, cooked vegetables) on top as desired. Lightly season with salt and pepper. Cook briefly until set and golden underneath. Do not overcook. With spatula, fold the omelet in half so the fillings are inside. Slide the cooked omelet onto a plate.

BEANS

Nutritious, dirt cheap and versatile in many tasty ways, cooked beans in cans or jars are available in many varieties (black, red, white, pinto, navy, etc.). It takes time to cook them from scratch but they simmer quietly while you are busy with something else. Cooked beans refrigerate and freeze well and provide the basis for quick and cheap meals. You can use just a small portion as needed.

BUYING AND STORING BEANS: Dry beans are sold packaged or in bulk at supermarkets, open air markets, health food stores, specialty stores, and ethnic stores. Store dried beans tightly covered in a cool, dry place.

SOAKING? Recent research by some bean experts suggests that presoaking may not be necessary and does not make the beans noticeably easier to digest. Mexicans and Jamaicans, who use lots of beans, do not presoak them. As for digestive concerns, cook beans very well until tender and eat them more often, at first in smaller quantities, to develop a healthy tolerance to beans' sugars and fiber. If you wish to soak the beans, choose long soak or quick soak. **Long soak:** Cover dried, rinsed beans with four times their volume of cold water and soak for 8-24 hours. Drain, discard water, rinse and cook in fresh water (see below). **Quick soak:** In large saucepan, cover dried, rinsed beans with four times their volume of cold water. Bring to a boil, uncovered, then remove from heat and let stand covered for one hour. Drain, discard the water, rinse and cook in fresh water (see below).

COOKING BEANS: Pick over dry beans to discard any debris, rinse and drain (presoak if desired). In a large saucepan or soup pot, bring lots of water to full boil (about four times the quantity of dried beans). Add the beans, bring to second boil without cover. Reduce the heat to low, cover & simmer for 1-1/2 to 2-1/2 hours until tender; check occasionally and add a little more water if needed. Cooking time depends on the size and type of beans, on how long they have been stored, and whether or not they have been presoaked. Check for doneness by tasting to make sure the beans are **soft and tender.** One cup of dried beans yields 2-3 cups of cooked beans. Cover and refrigerate cooked beans for 5 days (in the remaining cooking liquid so they won't dry out). Use cooked beans in recipes instead of canned beans. Or divide into serving portions (with some of the cooking liquid) and freeze in small containers or freezer-strength, self-sealing plastic bags for up to 3 months.

GREAT BEAN RECIPES:

Pasta

Wonderful pasta comes in many varieties such as fettuccine, spaghetti, ziti, macaroni, noodles, rotini, fusilli. Cheap, versatile and filling, pasta makes a fast, easy, and delicious meal. Cook enough to last for several days. Cover & refrigerate leftovers for up to 3-5 days, or freeze for up to three months.

COOKING PASTA: Use a large saucepan or soup pot with lots of water so the pasta can move around freely and there is plenty of room for bubbling water. Cover the pot and bring water to full boil, then add a teaspoon of salt and all the pasta at once. (Do not add oil to the cooking water because it makes the pasta slippery and the sauce won't stick to it.) To prevent the pasta from sticking, stir it immediately until water returns to boil; reduce the heat a bit if necessary to prevent the water from boiling over. Cook uncovered for 8-12 minutes (according to package); do not overcook. Drain immediately so the cooked pasta doesn't get soggy and slimy, then put it back into the saucepan, toss thoroughly with sauce, or set aside to use in recipes.

The fastest way to savor hot pasta is to add a small lump of butter and grated Parmesan (or other cheese) on top.

REHEATING PASTA. Microwave: Add one tablespoon of water to a small bowlful of pasta, and heat at medium high (80%) for 3 minutes. Or spoon pasta sauce and/or grated cheese over pasta, cover and heat for 3 minutes. **Stovetop:** Add a little bit of water to the pasta in saucepan, cover and simmer over medium low heat for several minutes until hot. Or heat it in vegetable steamer in saucepan with some boiling water underneath. **Regular oven:** Put pasta in ovenproof casserole, add a few spoonfuls of water, cover and bake for 15-20 minutes at 350°F (175°C).

GREAT PASTA RECIPES:

Baked ziti .... page 74
Chunky pasta sauce .... page 40
Creamy corn casserole .... page 74
Creamy pasta veggie combo .... page 78
Egg noodles à la Rina .... page 40
Italian spaghetti sauce .... page 85
Macaroni and cheese casserole .... page 76
Meat & macaroni casserole .... page 67
Minestrone soup .... page 55
Pasta Alfredo for one .... page 40
Pasta frittata .... page 43
Pasta salad .... page 48

Potatoes

Potatoes are cheap, tasty, versatile, high in nutrition and fibre, and low in fat. Buy in small quantities (for 7-10 days) and store in a cool, dark, ventilated place if possible, away from light. When cooking/baking potatoes, peel them very thinly, or scrub well and also eat the nutritious and delicious peel.

MICROWAVING POTATOES: Scrub potatoes. Do not pierce them; the skin is porous enough and will not explode while the steam bakes the potato. **One potato:** Place it on a paper towel on microwave floor, bake at full power for about 3-5 minutes, wrap in towel and let stand for 3 minutes. **Several potatoes:** Spread them out in a wheel pattern, and bake at full power: 2 potatoes for 5-8 minutes; 3 potatoes for 7-10 minutes; 4 potatoes for 10-12 minutes. Wrap baked potatoes in a towel and let stand for about 5 minutes to continue baking. The potato should yield to gentle touch when ready. Slit top open and spread apart, add fillings like sour cream, chopped broccoli, cottage cheese or shredded mozzarella, and simulated bacon bits (made from soy beans, they are inexpensive and delicious). Season with a sprinkle of salt and pepper or with herb mix.

BOILING POTATOES: Red or white potatoes are good for boiling. The best way to boil them is in their skins in a small amount of water to keep nutrients from escaping. Scrub potatoes, put them in a saucepan, add water (2 cups or 500 mL) and bring to a boil. The water does not have to cover the potatoes if your saucepan is tightly covered so the steam can work its magic, but check occasionally to see that the water doesn't completely dry out. Reduce the heat to medium low and cook, tightly covered, until tender, for about 45 minutes to 1 hour. Test with fork. Drain. (Cover with lid to keep the drained potatoes hot for 30 minutes.)

BAKED POTATOES: Long russet or "Idaho" potatoes are great for baking. Whenever you use your oven, throw in a few potatoes so they bake on the side, then store them in the refrigerator for a quick meal. You can bake potatoes alone or along with other food in the oven (such as casseroles) to take advantage of the heat. Preheat oven to 350-400°F (175-200°C). Thoroughly wash and dry potatoes. Do not pierce the skin; the potatoes will not explode since the skin is porous enough, and the steam cooks the potato. Place the potatoes directly on the oven rack and bake for 1 hour or more until tender when tested with fork, or when they yield to gentle pressure. For crusty potatoes, rub skin lightly with vegetable oil before baking. Cut hot potato top crosswise, squeeze it slightly apart, top with some butter or sour cream, chives, cheese, simulated bacon bits or herb mix and enjoy. The potato skin is the best part.

Cooked potatoes are tasty hot or cold. Scandinavian-style herring or dried, salted fish goes well with them. Stir-fry cold leftover potatoes in bite-size chunks in a little butter, season with salt and pepper. Béchamel sauce (page 92) mixed with crushed, hard-boiled eggs and seasoned with salt and pepper makes a delicious sauce for baked or cooked potatoes. Brown gravy (page 86) is an old-fashioned and soul-satisfying sauce for hot, cooked potatoes.

GREAT POTATO RECIPES:

Baked potato skins .... page 71
Barley soup .... page 52
Broccoli potatoes............ page 77
Corn potato chowder ..... page 52
Creamy potato soup .... page 52
Kielbasa casserole .... page 64
Leek and potato soup..... page 53
Mashed potatoes .... page 70
Potato frittata .... page 77
Potato patties .... page 70
Roasted vegetables .... page 75
Scalloped potatoes .... page 41

RICE

Rice is cheap and versatile and can be used in many delicious recipes. It stretches any meal and you only need small quantities of meat or chicken if any. The recipes in this book use mostly long-grain rice. Basmati rice is great for pilafs. Cooking regular rice takes only 20 minutes total. It's easy to learn to cook perfect rice.

BUYING AND STORING: Rice is available at supermarkets, ethnic markets and health food stores. It is cheapest in bulk or in big bags. Store it in a closed container in a dry place.

COOKING WHITE LONG-GRAIN RICE OR CONVERTED RICE: Measure carefully for perfect rice. In saucepan with tight-fitting lid, bring to full boil 2 cups (500 mL) of water. Add 1/2 tsp (2 mL) salt and 1 cup (250 mL) rice. Stir once, reduce heat to minimum, cover tightly and simmer for 17-20 minutes. Do not peek or stir while the rice is cooking. All the water will be absorbed. Remove it from heat, immediately fluff the rice with fork, then cover again and let stand for 5 minutes. Keeps hot for 30 minutes. Makes 3 cups (750 mL) of cooked rice. (Cooked rice is tasty as is, or sprinkle it with a little soy sauce.)

COOKING BROWN RICE: To remove any dirt, rinse brown rice in a strainer until water runs clear. Cook as white rice above but simmer for 40 minutes.

MICROWAVE COOKING WHITE LONG-GRAIN RICE: Stovetop cooking of rice doesn't take any longer than microwaving and has a better taste. Yet, sometimes microwave cooking is practical so here are the instructions: Put 2 cups (500 mL) of water in an 8-cup (2 L) microwavable bowl, and bring to a boil (5 minutes at full power). Add 1 cup (250 mL) of rice and 1/2 tsp (2 mL) of salt. Stir, cover tightly and cook for 10 minutes at 30% (medium low). Stir and cook for another 10 minutes at 30% (medium low). Let stand for 5 minutes. Fluff it with fork and serve immediately.

REFRIGERATING AND FREEZING COOKED RICE: Cooking time remains the same even if you make a double or triple batch of rice. If you plan to serve the rice with a fabulous sauce, leave the salt out of the cooking water. Make enough rice for several days since it keeps well in the refrigerator for up to 5-6 days. Or divide it into small quantities and freeze in freezer-strength self-sealing plastic bags for up to 6-8 months, then defrost/reheat in the microwave oven whenever you need rice in a hurry.

REHEATING RICE: In a saucepan, stir cold rice with a fork, add a spoonful or two of water underneath the rice, cover tightly and heat over very low heat for several minutes. Or sprinkle with water, cover and microwave at 80% (medium high heat) for 3 minutes until hot.

RINSING? It depends on source, type and desired degree of stickiness. Rinsing is not necessary for domestic, plain long-grain rice (that's rice from North American sources) or converted rice (check the package). If you buy imported long-grain rice, rinse it before cooking to remove the starch; otherwise your rice will be sticky. To rinse rice, place it in a strainer and run cold water over it until water runs clear. On the other hand, when you want rice to stick together so it can be eaten with chopsticks, buy imported rice and do not rinse it. For risotto or pilaf, use short-grain rice, aromatic Basmati, or Italian Arborio, and do not rinse it before cooking because you want to retain the starches to make the dish creamy.

GREAT RICE RECIPES:

Baked rice pilaf .... page 70
Bean tofu burgers .... page 73
Beans & rice .... page 39
Caribbean rice & ham..... page 64
Chinese fried rice............ page 72
Curry chicken.................. page 60
Humble rice bake .... page 44
Lentil soup .... page 56
Rich rice.......................... page 71
Stovetop rice and meat .. page 63
Tofu risotto .... page 78
Tropical beans................. page 81

Minute Meals, Midnight Snacks, Microwave Miracles

It's good to have a meal ready and waiting for reheating when you come home hungry. Plan ahead for busy, hungry times so you'll have basics and leftovers in your refrigerator and the meal is virtually done. Freeze extra portions of rice and beans, casseroles and soups, in small containers or freezer-strength, self-sealing plastic bags.

Absolutely do not miss "BASICS" (eggs, beans, pasta, potatoes, rice) on pages 29-36. Cold sandwiches (page 28), salads (46), sweet stuff (110), milkshakes (117) and other beverages (116) & many vegetarian meals (70) take just minutes.

This icon signals fast recipes in other categories.

TORTILLA PIZZAS

Prep: 2 minutes per pizza. Bake: 5 minutes.

Super easy and popular with friends. Thin flour tortilla bakes into a crispy crust in hot oven. Fold pizza in half for lunch-to-go, put in self-sealing plastic bag and eat cold or heat in microwave.

Flour tortillas
Pasta sauce in jar
Shredded cheese (mozzarella, Gouda, Monterey Jack or cheddar)

Preheat oven to 450°F (230°C). On baking sheet, place tortillas side-by-side. Spread pasta sauce and shredded cheese on each tortilla. Bake for 5 minutes.

Variations: Add olives, onions, mushrooms, sliced salami etc. if desired. Or use large thin pita bread, or Italian-style Platina flatbread; bake Platina for 8 minutes.

RICH NACHOS

Prep: 2 minutes. Microwave: 5 minutes (or bake in regular oven: 10 minutes).

A tasty snack anytime. Always popular for the gang.

Tortilla chips
Salsa
Shredded cheese (mozzarella or cheddar)
(Optional: Pitted olives, canned red kidney beans)

Spread tortilla chips on large microwavable plate. Spread some salsa over chips and top evenly with handful of cheese. Microwave at 70% (medium high heat) for 5 minutes until cheese is melted and bubbly. (If you use olives and beans, spread them over chips before adding salsa and cheese.) Or bake in regular oven at 400°F (200°C) for 10 minutes.

Corn-On-The-Cob

Cook: 4 minutes.

Easy cooking for summertime when corn is fresh and plentiful.

Whout husking, place a fresh ear of corn on a sheet or two of paper toweling in microwave. Microwave at 100% (full power) for 4 minutes. Let stand for 1 minute. Pull the husk and silks away and your meal is ready. Fabulous as is, or add butter and salt if desired.

Bean Burritos

Prep: 5 minutes. Cook: 6 minutes (or bake: 10 minutes, or microwave: 30 seconds). 1-2 servings.

2	Flour tortillas	2
1/2 cup	Cooked or canned beans (red, black or pinto), drained, crushed lightly with fork	125 mL
4 tbsp	Pasta sauce (or salsa)	60 mL
1/2 cup	Shredded cheese	125 mL

Optional: Add leftover meat, chicken, veggies to filling.

Place tortillas on countertop. Spread crushed beans in the middle of tortillas edge-to-edge, cover with pasta sauce, top with cheese. Roll each tortilla into a log. Put the logs in ungreased frying pan, cover and cook over medium high heat for 3 minutes. Turn logs over, cover and cook for 3 more minutes so logs get slightly brown and hot and the cheese melts. (Or bake at 400°F/200°C) for 10 minutes. Or wrap in waxed paper and microwave each burrito at full power for 30 seconds.) **Hawaiian touch:** Add pineapple tidbits to the filling.

Beans & Rice

Mix some cooked or canned beans with cooked rice, add pasta sauce (or salsa or HP Sauce) and shredded cheese on top, season with herbs etc. and heat until cheese melts. Makes a good microwavable lunch. (Page 36: Cooking rice.)

Bean Spread

Drain 1 cup (250 mL) of canned red beans, crush with fork. Combine with small chopped onion, chopped tomato, crushed hard-boiled egg, handful of chopped fresh parsley, vegetable oil & salt & pepper to taste. Mix coarsely with fork. Eat with pita or other bread. Filling, delicious, nutritious & easy.

Fried Beans

Heat a little oil in frying pan. Add one chopped onion and 2-3 grated garlic cloves. Stir-fry over medium high heat for 2 minutes. Add cooked or canned beans (pinto beans are great), season with salt, pepper & cumin powder, stir-fry until lightly browned and tender crisp. (Add some cooking liquid from the beans, chopped tomatoes and cheese if desired.) Fried beans are delicious as is, hot or cold. Or use them for recipes in this book. **(Easy & practical: Freezing and grating whole garlic cloves, see page 80.)**

Egg Noodles À La Rina

Cook medium egg noodles (see page 33 for cooking pasta), drain and return to saucepan. While the noodles are still hot, add a splash of chicken bouillon liquid concentrate (Bovril®)*, soy sauce and oil, and sprinkle with herb mix (Mrs. Dash® or Spike®). Stir and eat immediately. (*To substitute, microwave 1/2 bouillon cube in spoonful of water for 30 seconds, stir well.)

Pasta Alfredo For One

Instead of traditional fettuccine, use noodles which are easier to cook and eat. Cook two handfuls of medium egg noodles for 10 minutes, drain and return to saucepan. Over medium high heat, add a small lump of butter to noodles and sprinkle with black pepper. Stir for a minute. Drizzle a few tablespoons of light cream (15% or "half-and-half") on top, sprinkle with grated Parmesan cheese and stir until hot and creamy, for 2-3 minutes. Eat immediately.

Chunky Pasta Sauce

Prepared pasta sauce in large jars is versatile, inexpensive and delicious. It is more practical than canned sauces because you can use just a bit as needed and refrigerate the rest in the original jar. While your pasta is cooking, make this sauce. Heat a little oil in frying pan, add chopped/sliced, raw vegetables (onions, zucchini, tomatoes, green peppers, mushrooms, garlic, celery) and stir-fry over medium high heat for several minutes until tender crisp. Add pasta sauce, bring to a boil, reduce the heat, cover and simmer for 5 minutes. Freeze extra portions. (Add stir-fried ground meat for meat-veggie version.)

Mexican Melts

Slice a crusty bun, spread with crushed beans (cooked, canned or fried) and top with shredded cheese. Bake at 450°F (230°C) for 10 minutes.

Scalloped Potatoes For One

Prep: 5 minutes. Microwave: 13-15 minutes. 1 serving.

This potato-lover's microwave recipe satisfies your late-night hunger.

1 tbsp	**Butter**	**15 mL**
3 tbsp	**All-purpose flour**	**45 mL**
1 cup	**Water**	**250 mL**
1	**Cube or sachet of vegetable or chicken bouillon**	**1**
2	**Medium potatoes**	**2**
1	**Small onion**	**1**

In large measuring cup (4 cups or 1 L), microwave butter at 100% for 30 seconds so it melts. Stir in flour until smooth, add water and bouillon cube. Microwave at 100% for 2 minutes, stir. Microwave for another 2 minutes, stir. Meanwhile, scrub potatoes well and slice them thinly and uniformly (so they will cook evenly). Slice onion. Layer sliced potatoes and onion in microwavable casserole, pour sauce all over. Cover and microwave at 100% for 13-15 minutes until very tender; stir once or twice during cooking. (Let stand for 3 minutes.)

Hot Russian Sandwich

Total time: 10 minutes.

Black Russian bread is best for this indescribably satisfying mini-meal but other dark bread works well too.

Black bread, sliced thick
Pasta sauce in jar
Garlic cloves, sliced
Sliced cheese (mozzarella, Monterey Jack or cheddar)

Preheat oven to 425°F (220°). Toast bread slices and place them on a baking sheet, side-by-side. Spread a large spoonful of pasta sauce on each slice. Throw on several fresh garlic cloves, sliced. Cover generously with sliced cheese. Bake for 6-8 minutes until cheese bubbles and is golden brown.

Quick Quesadillas

This is a delicious, filling sandwich or lunch-to-go. On small corn tortillas, spread some cooked, crushed beans and shredded cheese (add salsa, onions, garlic, cumin, & chili powder if desired). Fold tortillas in half, heat in ungreased frying pan at medium high heat, flipping over until cheese melts. Eat hot or cold.

Zucchini Sauté

Prep: 5 minutes. Cook: 8-10 minutes. 2 servings.

If you have cooked rice in small bags in your freezer (see page 36), heat one in microwave while you make this delicious side dish.

2 tbsp	Vegetable oil	30 mL
1	Medium onion, sliced	1
4	Medium zucchini, unpeeled, sliced	4
1 tsp	Vegetable bouillon liquid concentrate (or microwave 1/2 cube in spoonful of water, stir to mix)	5 mL
1/2 tsp	Each dried granulated garlic and cumin powder	2 mL

Heat oil in frying pan over medium high heat. Add onion and zucchini, sprinkle with bouillon, garlic, and cumin. Cover, and simmer for 8-10 minutes over medium high heat, toss once or twice to distribute flavors.

Gourmet Melt

Total time: 10 minutes.

Impress someone special and serve this special treat as a late-night snack.

English muffin (or bagel)
Onion, tomato, avocado, all sliced
Cheese, sliced (soft goat cheese or Havarti is perfect, but use whatever you have around)

Preheat oven to 425°F (220°C). Split and toast English muffin (or bagel). Place the toasted halves on a baking sheet, cut sides up, side-by-side. Top each with sliced onion, tomato, avocado and then with cheese. Bake for 8 minutes until cheese bubbles and is golden brown. **(Keep leftover avocado green by rubbing lemon juice on cut surface and covering it tightly with plastic wrap. Refrigerate and use as soon as possible.)**

Pita Melts

Preheat oven to 400°F (200°C). Cut pita in quarters and fill with sliced cheese (mozzarella, cheddar or similar). Bake for 5 minutes to make crispy, hot sandwiches. (Add leftover beans, ham, pepperoni or vegetables if desired.)

PASTA FRITTATA

Prep: 3 minutes. Microwave: 10 minutes (or stovetop: 13 minutes, or bake: 30 minutes). 2 generous servings.

Frittata is like a crustless quiche or thick omelet except you leave it flat. It is a great encore dish for all your leftover pasta (spaghetti, fettuccine, egg noodles, cut macaroni or fusilli). Even overcooked, gluey pasta can be used; just cut it into small pieces with a knife first. The milk-egg mixture will bond the ingredients so you can cut the cooked frittata into wedges. Equally tasty hot or cold; refrigerate leftovers. Make a lot for a week's lunches.

3 cups	**Cooked pasta, hot or cold**	**750 mL**
2	**Large eggs**	**2**
3/4 cup	**Milk**	**180 mL**
1/2 cup	**Shredded cheese (mozzarella, cheddar or similar)**	**125 mL**
	Salt and black pepper to taste	
	(Optional: Leftover vegetables, ham, cooked meat or sausage)	

Microwave directions: Grease microwavable pie plate and spread pasta in it. Beat eggs and milk with fork, add cheese, salt and pepper (and other ingredients). Pour the mixture all over the pasta. Microwave at 100% (full power) for 10 minutes until set. Let sit for 2 minutes.

Frying pan: Heat a little butter in frying pan. Mix all the ingredients and spread evenly all over the bottom. Cook over medium heat for 5-8 minutes until nicely browned underneath. Slide onto a large plate, browned side down, then flip over and brown the other side.

Oven: Bake in a greased pie plate at 350°F (175°C) for 30 minutes.

MELBA MELTS

Microwave (at 50%): 1 melt for 30 seconds, 3 melts for 1 minute.

Brew a pot of tea and make a pile of these delicious snacks. For each melt, sandwich a thin slice of cheese (mozzarella, cheddar or similar) between 2 slices of multigrain Melba toast, put them on a small plate or a sheet of waxed paper and microwave at 50% (medium heat) until cheese melts. Do not overcook. (Try other breads. All Scandinavian-style crisp, thin breads such as Kavli, Wasa, Ryvita, Finncrisp etc. and also sliced bun-type crisp breads like Olof work well for this fast sandwich. Kavli is almost paper-thin so make double-deckers with three slices of bread with sliced cheese in between.)

Grilled Cheese Sandwich

Total time: 8-10 minutes.

Perennial favorite for kids and adults alike. A tasty breakfast, lunch or snack anytime.

Butter
Two slices of bread
Cheese (mozzarella, cheddar or processed cheese)

Heat frying pan to medium high. Toast the bread slices if they are very soft. Lightly butter one side of each slice. Put one slice in frying pan, buttered side down, top with sliced cheese and then with remaining bread slice, buttered side up. Cook until crisp and golden underneath, about 3 minutes. Press the sandwich down gently with spatula (or flat plate) while it is frying to better melt the cheese. Flip it over with spatula and fry the other side. Cut diagonally. **Delicious variation:** Use peanut butter instead of cheese and grill or fry the sandwich as above; let cool before cutting it in half.

Eat-Them-Like-Fries

Total time: 10 minutes.

Buy a bagful of really fresh beans and simmer them to give you edible company while studying.

Green beans or yellow wax beans
Melted butter or vegetable oil
Lemon juice (fresh or bottled)
Grated fresh garlic or dried granulated garlic

Rinse beans and snip ends off. In large saucepan, boil 1 cup of water. Add beans, reduce the heat, cover and simmer for 5 minutes until tender crisp (do not overcook), drain. Drizzle cooked, hot beans with a little melted butter or oil, sprinkle lemon juice and garlic all over.

Humble Rice Bake

Total time: 5 minutes. 1 serving.

Put one serving of cooked leftover rice (or baked rice pilaf) in microwavable bowl. Add two tablespoons of pasta sauce. Spread some grated cheese on top. Microwave for 2 minutes at full power.

The microwavable recipes in this book have been tested on a 700W model. Other models with different wattage may require a little more or less cooking time.

SALADS

Sunshine Salad

Total time: 10 minutes. 2 servings.

4	Carrots	4
1	Orange	1
2 tbsp	Lemon juice	30 mL

Grate carrots. Peel orange with knife and also remove thin white layer between peel and flesh. Then, with your knife, separate each pocket and remove flesh only and chop into small chunks. Combine carrots and orange pieces in a bowl, squeeze orange juice (from remaining orange parts) and lemon juice on top.

Quick Potato Salad

In bowl, mix three large spoonfuls each of plain yogurt and mayonnaise. Season with black pepper and salt. Add five or six chilled, cooked, cubed potatoes, two stalks of celery and medium red onion (both sliced), two dill pickles, green apple, and green pepper (all diced). Toss everything together and garnish generously with chopped fresh dill or parsley.

Colorful Coleslaw For One

Total time: 10 minutes. 1 serving.

Easy and fast, simply delicious. If you wish to make it Slim Slaw, use low-fat yogurt and low-fat mayonnaise for dressing.

1/2 cup	Shredded red cabbage	125 mL
1/2 cup	Shredded green cabbage	125 mL
1	Small carrot, grated	1
1/2	Small green pepper, chopped	1/2
1 tbsp	Plain yogurt	15 mL
1 tsp	Mayonnaise	5 mL
1/4 tsp	Dijon mustard	1 mL

Toss cabbage, carrot and green pepper together in a small bowl. Stir yogurt together with mayonnaise and mustard, pour on top and toss.

Rice Salad

Combine cold leftover rice (converted or long-grain is best because it separates well), diced apple, shredded carrot, and a small can of corn (drained). Season with salt, sugar & lemon juice. Mix in plain yogurt and a dollop of mayonnaise.

Coleslaw For A Crowd

Prep: 15 minutes. Makes 6 generous servings.

Double or triple the recipe if you have a big crowd. The dressing for this popular salad is so tasty and creamy that you can also use it as a dip for chips and raw vegetables.

4 cups	Cabbage, shredded	1 L
1	Medium onion, chopped	1
1	Green pepper, chopped	1
1/2 cup	Whipping cream, 35%	125 mL
1/2 cup	Sour cream	125 mL
1 tbsp	Dijon mustard	15 mL
2 tsp	Lemon juice	10 mL
1 tbsp	Sugar	15 mL
1/2 tsp each	Salt and black pepper	2 mL each

In large bowl, combine cabbage, onion and green pepper. In small bowl, whisk together remaining ingredients until well blended. Pour over cabbage and toss. (Chill for one hour if time allows.)

Bean Salad

Prep: 10 minutes. 10 servings.

This is an old favorite, great for a hungry crowd. It goes well with hot or cold, plain rice. Nutritious and filling. Keeps 3 days in refrigerator.

1/3 cup	Vegetable oil	75 mL
3 tbsp	Red wine vinegar	45 mL
2 tbsp	Lemon juice	30 mL
1 tsp	Salt	5 mL
1/2 tsp	Black pepper	2 mL
1 tbsp	Brown sugar	15 mL
1 can each (14 oz.)	Cut green beans, yellow wax beans, chickpeas, red kidney beans, white beans (all rinsed and drained)	1 can each (398 mL)
3	Celery stalks, sliced	3
1 each	Green pepper, red pepper, large red onion, all chopped	1 each

In large bowl, whisk together oil, vinegar, lemon juice, salt, pepper and sugar. Add remaining ingredients, toss to coat. Chill if time allows.

Pasta Salad

Prep: 15 minutes. 6 servings.

Light yet filling meal. (To cook pasta, see page 33.)

3 tbsp each	Olive oil, red wine vinegar, lemon juice	45 mL each
1	Garlic clove, grated	1
3 cups	Cooked small spiral pasta (fusilli) or macaroni, chilled	750 mL
3	Stalks celery, diced	3
1	Green pepper, chopped	1
1 cup	Diced cucumber	250 mL
1	Medium red onion, chopped	1
1/2 cup	Stuffed olives (halved)	125 mL
	Salt and black pepper to taste	

To make dressing, whisk together oil, vinegar, lemon juice and grated garlic in small bowl. In large bowl, stir together remaining ingredients. Pour salad dressing on top and toss. Season to taste with salt and pepper. (If desired, add chopped hard-boiled eggs, diced apple and/or diced cheese.)

Couscous Salad

Total time: 15 minutes. 4-6 servings.

1 cup	Couscous	250 mL
1 cup	Boiling water	250 mL
3 tbsp	Olive oil	45 mL
2 tbsp	Lemon juice	30 mL
2 tbsp	Vegetable oil	30 mL
1	Large onion, chopped	1
3	Tomatoes, chopped	3
1 cup	Chopped fresh parsley	250 mL
2 tbsp	Fresh mint leaves, chopped	30 mL
	Salt and black pepper to taste	

In large measuring cup or small bowl, pour boiling water over couscous. Add olive oil and lemon juice. Stir and let stand for 3 minutes. Fluff with fork and chill for 10 minutes while you make the rest of the salad. Meanwhile, heat vegetable oil in frying pan and stir-fry onion for 3 minutes over medium high heat. In large bowl, mix all ingredients, including couscous and onion. Season with salt and pepper. Fluff thoroughly with fork.

(Another great couscous recipe with veggies and tofu is on page 89.)

TUNA SALAD

Prep: 10 minutes. 1-2 servings.

Use tuna salad as sandwich filler for toast or pita.

1 can	**Water-packed tuna (6 oz. / 170 g) drained, flaked with fork**	**1 can**
1	**Stalk celery, chopped finely**	**1**
1	**Small onion, minced**	**1**
4 tbsp	**Mayonnaise**	**60 mL**
	Black pepper (or lemon pepper) to taste	

In small bowl, combine all ingredients. Stir until well blended.

GREEK SALAD

Prep: 10 minutes.

The quantities are flexible so just follow your taste.

Romaine lettuce
Tomatoes, cut into chunks
Green pepper, sliced thinly
Cucumber, sliced
Red onion, sliced thinly into rings
Handful of black olives (Kalamata)
Olive oil
Lemon juice
Salt and black pepper to taste
Handful of feta cheese (chunks)

Rinse and dry lettuce, tear into pieces and arrange on large platter or in large shallow bowl. Add tomatoes, pepper, cucumber and onion rings. Top with olives. Drizzle a bit of oil on top, then lemon juice, then sprinkle gently with salt and pepper. Spread feta chunks all over. (Add croutons if desired, see page 58.)

EASY SALAD

Prep: 10 minutes.

Combine diced tomatoes, cucumber, green pepper and red onion in bowl. Drizzle a little olive oil on top, sprinkle with lemon juice, season with salt and pepper to taste. Toss to mix.

Salad Dressings

A bewildering variety of bottled salad dressings is available at supermarkets but it's easy and fun to make your own "secret house dressing." Save small glass jars with lids from jams etc. to shake and store your dressings. Here are a few easy, basic ones to get you started. Quantities and ingredients are flexible, so feel free to improvise and let your taste be your guide. When you use salad greens, tomatoes, cucumbers etc. in salad, add dressing only to the portion you'll eat right away; refrigerate leftover salad and dressing separately for your next meal.

Put all ingredients in small jar, cover, shake to blend well. Or use a small bowl and whisk ingredients together. Refrigerate leftover salad dressings.

French (basic vinaigrette): 6 parts olive oil, 3 parts red wine vinegar, 1 part Dijon mustard. Season with grated garlic clove, salt & black pepper.	**Creamy vinaigrette:** 8 parts plain yogurt, 2 parts each of red wine vinegar & olive oil, 1 part each of lemon juice & Dijon mustard. Garlic, black pepper, salt to taste.
Tomato: As basic vinaigrette above, but use ketchup instead of mustard & garlic.	**Creamy Honey Mustard:** 8 parts light cream, 1 part Dijon mustard, 1 part honey. Salt and pepper to taste. (Liquidy, sweet.)
Lemon: 3 parts olive oil, 1 part fresh lemon juice, salt and pepper to taste. (If desired, season with grated garlic cloves, minced basil or chives or dill...)	**Low-fat yogurt & lemon:** 2 parts plain low-fat yogurt, 1 part fresh lemon juice. Add a dash of brown sugar, season to taste with salt and black pepper. (Sweet.)
Easy Chef: 2 parts olive oil, 2 parts sour cream, 1 part red wine vinegar. Add sprinkling of "Chef's Salad" spice to taste.	**Low-fat creamy:** 2 parts each plain yogurt and buttermilk, 1 part fresh lemon juice. Salt and lemon pepper to taste. (Tart.)
Blue cheese: 4 parts each plain yogurt & olive oil, 2 parts wine vinegar, 1 part each crumbled blue cheese & cream cheese, black pepper to taste. (Thick, rich.)	**Low-low-low-cal "Italian":** A splash of V8 juice or Garden Cocktail, that's all. Delicious.

Soups

Creamy Potato Soup For Two

Prep: 5 minutes. Total time: 20 minutes. 2 servings.

2	Medium potatoes, grated	2
1	Small onion, minced	1
1 cup	Water	250 mL
1 cube	Vegetable bouillon	1 cube
1 cup	Milk	250 mL
1 tsp	Soy sauce	5 mL
2 tbsp	All-purpose flour	30 mL
1 tbsp	Butter	15 mL

In medium saucepan, combine grated potatoes, onion, water and bouillon cube and bring to a boil. Reduce heat to medium, cover and simmer for 10 minutes. In small bowl or measuring cup, stir together milk, soy sauce and flour until smooth. Stir the mixture into the soup, then add butter (and a little more water if needed). Cover and simmer over medium heat for 5 minutes.

Corn Potato Chowder

Use the recipe above but make two changes. Dice the potatoes instead of grating them and add a small can of creamed corn.

Barley Soup

Prep: 10 minutes. Total time: 1 hour. 4 servings.

Easy, cheap and soul-satisfying on a cold winter's day.

1 tbsp	Vegetable oil	15 mL
1	Medium onion, chopped	1
1	Medium potato, diced	1
1	Medium carrot, diced	1
1/4 cup	Pot barley (pearl barley)	60 mL
3 cups	Water	750 mL
2 cubes	Vegetable bouillon	2 cubes
Dash	Black pepper	Dash
1/2 tsp	Dried granulated garlic	2 mL
1 tbsp	Soy sauce	15 mL

In large saucepan, heat oil. Sauté onion for 2 minutes over medium high heat. Add remaining ingredients. Bring to a boil. Reduce the heat to medium low, cover and simmer for 45 minutes. (Add a bit more water if too thick.)

LEEK AND POTATO SOUP

Prep: 10 minutes. Cook: 30 minutes. 2 servings.

Simple and light. Rinse leek rings well after slicing them to remove any grit from between the layers.

1 tbsp	Vegetable oil	15 mL
1	Leek, sliced & rinsed well	1
2	Potatoes, peeled, diced	2
3	Green onions, sliced (or one small onion, chopped)	3
1	Carrot, peeled, diced	1
4 cups	Water	1 L
2 cubes	Vegetable bouillon	2 cubes
	Salt and pepper to taste	

In large saucepan, heat oil, add leek and sauté for 3 minutes. Add remaining ingredients, bring to a boil. Turn heat to low, cover and simmer for 25 minutes.

CHEESE SOUP

Total time: 20 minutes. 6 servings.

Velvety smooth and satisfying. If you have "Bagel Bits" (page 95) or croutons (page 58) around, drop some into your bowl.

3 tbsp	Butter	45 mL
4 tbsp	All-purpose flour	60 mL
2	Medium onions, chopped	2
3 cups	Water	750 mL
3 cubes	Vegetable bouillon	3 cubes
4 oz.	Cream cheese (or grated cheddar)	125 g
1 cup	Milk	250 mL
2 tsp each	Salt and sugar	10 mL each

In soup pot, melt butter. Add flour and onions and stir-fry for 3 minutes over medium high heat. Add water and bouillon cubes, turn heat to high and bring to a boil, stirring constantly. Reduce heat to medium low and cook uncovered for 5 minutes, stirring frequently. Add cheese, turn heat to medium high and stir with whisk until cheese melts and the soup is hot. Add milk, salt and sugar, heat but do not let boil. (Decorate each bowl with some grated carrots, minced parsley or chives, sliced green onions or grated cheese if desired.)

Variation: Add canned corn, fresh or frozen chopped vegetables (broccoli or spinach, cauliflower, mushrooms, peas or green beans etc.) and/or cooked macaroni for a chunky cheese soup.

French Onion Soup

Prep: 15 minutes. Cook and bake: 40 minutes. 6 servings.

Always classy and popular, especially on a cold winter's night. It's easier than you think to make it from scratch. Use any old bread you have around.

3 tbsp	Butter	45 mL
4	Large yellow onions, thinly sliced	4
2 tbsp	All-purpose flour	30 mL
1/4 tsp	Black pepper	1 mL
5 cups	Water	1,25 L
4 cubes	Beef bouillon*	4 cubes
	Worchestershire sauce to taste	
6 slices	French or Italian bread, thickly sliced and toasted	6 slices
	Several garlic cloves, grated	
	Shredded cheese (Gruyère or Swiss)	

**Variation: Instead of beef bouillon, use chicken cubes plus sautéed mushrooms.*

Melt butter in soup pot over medium high heat. Add onions and cook for 10 minutes, stirring frequently, until softened and golden brown. Sprinkle with flour and pepper and stir-fry for 2 minutes. Stir in water and bouillon cubes. Bring to a boil over high heat. Reduce heat to low, cover and simmer for 20 minutes. Check the taste and season with additional salt, pepper and a splash of Worchestershire sauce if desired. Preheat oven to 450°F (230°C). Pour soup into large ovenproof casserole (or individual ovenproof soup bowls), float toasted or dried bread slices on top side-by-side, sprinkle with grated garlic and cover generously with shredded cheese. Bake for about five minutes until cheese bubbles and is golden brown. Serve immediately.

Quick version: Use dry onion soup mix and dried granulated garlic instead of fresh onions and garlic.

LEMONS: Before they get old and dry, cut lemons in half and freeze in a small plastic bag. Defrost in the microwave and squeeze when you need lemon juice.

If your jar lid refuses to open, turn the jar upside down and bang the lid flat against a solid surface (countertop or floor); one bang is usually all it takes. Or place the end of a spoon under the lid and press down until you hear the vacuum seal release.

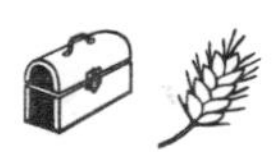

Minestrone Soup

Prep: 10 minutes. Total time: 30 minutes. 8 servings.

This Italian soup of vegetables and pasta makes a satisfying meal.

2 tbsp	Vegetable oil	30 mL
1	Large onion, chopped	1
6	Garlic cloves, minced	6
1 can	Diced tomatoes (about 2 cups or 500 mL)	1 can
1	Each celery stalk, medium zucchini, carrot, all diced	1
1 can	Red kidney beans, rinsed, drained (2 cups or 500 mL)	1 can
6 cups	Water	1.5 L
3 cubes	Vegetable bouillon	3 cubes
1 tsp each	Dried basil and oregano	5 mL each
	Dash Tabasco sauce	
1 cup	Small cut macaroni, uncooked	250 mL
	(Shredded cheese)	

Heat oil in large soup pot. Add onion and garlic and sauté for 3 minutes over medium high heat. Add remaining ingredients except macaroni. Bring to a boil over high heat. Add macaroni, reduce heat to medium low, cover and simmer for 15 minutes. (Garnish each bowl with shredded cheese.)

Cream Of Mushroom Soup

Total time: 20 minutes. 2 generous servings.

4 tbsp	Butter	60 mL
10-12 large	Fresh mushrooms, sliced (1 box, makes 2-3 cups sliced)	10-12 large
4 tbsp	All-purpose flour	60 mL
2-1/2 cups	Milk	625 mL
1 cube	Vegetable or chicken bouillon	1 cube
1 tsp	Soy sauce	5 mL

In large saucepan, melt butter. Add mushrooms and stir-fry for 5 minutes over medium high heat. Sprinkle flour all over. Stir-fry until no trace of flour remains. Add remaining ingredients. Stirring constantly with wire whisk to make the soup smooth and to prevent it from burning, bring to a boil. Reduce heat to medium and cook uncovered for 6 minutes, stirring frequently. If too thick, add a bit more milk.

Lentil Soup

Prep: 10 minutes. Cook: 1 hour. 6 servings.

Nutritious, filling. Use brown, red, yellow or green lentils.

2 tbsp	Vegetable oil	30 mL
1	Large onion, chopped	1
4	Garlic cloves, chopped	4
6 cups	Water	1.5 L
4 cubes	Vegetable bouillon	4 cubes
1/2 cup	Dried lentils	125 mL
1/4 cup	Uncooked rice	60 mL
2	Carrots, peeled and diced	2
1	Celery stalk, diced	1
3 tbsp	Soy sauce	45 mL
	Salt, pepper, dried basil to taste	

Pick over lentils to remove any grit, rinse and drain. In soup pot, heat oil, add onion and garlic and sauté for 3 minutes over medium high heat. Add remaining ingredients and bring to a boil over high heat. Reduce the heat to low, cover and simmer for 1 hour. Add a bit more water if the soup is too thick.

Vegetable Chowder

Prep: 10 minutes. Total time: 30 minutes. 8 servings.

This is a chunky, mild and delicious soup. Refrigerate leftovers quickly since this soup contains milk.

2 tbsp	Vegetable oil	30 mL
1	Large onion, chopped	1
4 tbsp	All-purpose flour	60 mL
1 tsp	Turmeric	5 mL
1 can	Corn, do not drain (12 oz. / 340 mL)	1
2 each	Medium carrots, potatoes, celery stalks, all diced	2 each
1 bunch	Broccoli, chopped	1 bunch
4 cups	Water	1 L
3 cubes	Vegetable bouillon	3 cubes
1-1/2 cups	Milk	375 mL

In soup pot, heat oil. Add onion, flour and turmeric, and stir-fry for 3 minutes over medium high heat. Add remaining ingredients except milk. Bring to a boil over high heat. Reduce heat to low, cover & simmer for 20 minutes. Add milk and heat but do not boil. (Sprinkle on some shredded cheese if desired.)

Seafood Chowder

Prep: 10 minutes. Total time: 20 minutes. 8 servings.

Chunky, delicious, easy meal. Eat with fresh bread. Refrigerate leftovers.

1/2 lb	Frozen fish fillets (sole, haddock or similar fish)	250 g
2 tbsp	Vegetable oil	30 mL
1	Medium onion, chopped	1
2	Celery stalks, sliced	2
1 can	Tomato soup (12 oz. or 340 mL), do not dilute	1 can
1 can	Commercial clam chowder (12 oz. / 340 mL), do not dilute	1 can
1 can	Corn (12 oz. / 340 mL)	1 can
1 tbsp	Soy sauce	15 mL
3 cups	Water	750 mL
1 cup	Milk	250 mL

Gourmet touch: Use mini-shrimp instead of fish.

Remove fish from carton and place in a large bowl of cold water to thaw partially. Meanwhile, heat oil in soup pot, and stir-fry onion for 2 minutes over medium high heat. Add remaining ingredients except milk, and bring to a boil. Cut partially defrosted fish into bite-size chunks and add to soup pot. Reduce heat to low, cover and simmer for 10 minutes. Add milk and heat but do not boil.

GINGERROOT: Scrub fresh gingerroot well and grate without peeling. Pick off larger bits of peel. Put grated leftovers into a self-sealing, strong plastic bag and spread out evenly into a thin layer. Freeze, then break off a piece as needed in recipes.

Herb mixtures (such as Mrs. Dash® or Spike®) are expensive but very practical and you only need a dash at a time. Consider making your own "house mixture" with your favorite herbs.

Bouillon concentrate: Bottled liquid concentrate (such as Bovril®) is a bit more expensive than cubes or powder but practical & delicious also as a seasoning. Saves time & trouble. You only use it by spoonfuls (and sometimes by drops). To substitute liquid concentrate for recipes without liquid where cube won't dissolve, microwave a cube in spoonful of water for 30 seconds, stir until smooth. (2 tsp = 1 cube = 1 sachet)

CHICKEN SOUP

Prep: 15 minutes. Cook: 1 hour. 6 servings.

This basic chicken soup will soothe your cold and winter blues. Keeps 3 days in the refrigerator.

2 tbsp	Vegetable oil	30 mL
1 lb	Drumsticks (or other pieces)	500 g
1	Large onion, chopped	1
	Salt and pepper to taste	
8 cups	Water	2 L
2 cubes	Chicken bouillon	2 cubes
2	Celery stalks, thinly sliced	2
2	Carrots, thinly sliced	2
2	Medium potatoes, diced	2
1 tbsp	Soy sauce	15 mL

Consider adding other ingredients, such as diced zucchini, rice, canned corn or beans (and extra water), to satisfy your taste or when you feed a crowd; or add a handful of extra-fine noodles minutes before soup is ready. Garnish with chopped green onions.

Heat oil in large soup pot over medium high heat. Add washed chicken pieces and onion, sprinkle with salt and pepper (go easy here, you can always add more later). Stir-fry for 8 minutes until nicely browned on each side. Add remaining ingredients, turn heat to high and bring to a boil uncovered. Reduce heat to medium low, cover and cook for 1 hour until tender.

Defatting cold or hot soup: When soup is refrigerated, the fat will congeal on the surface so you can easily remove it with a spoon if desired. Or, fill a freezer-strength self-sealing plastic bag with ice cubes and swish it on top of hot soup so the fat clings to the bag and can be lifted out and removed.

CROUTONS

OVEN: Preheat oven to 350°F (175°C). Cut stale or slightly dry bread slices into small cubes. Spread the cubes on a baking sheet in one layer. Bake for about 15 minutes until crusty and dry. Store in a canister or plastic bag.

FRYING PAN: Heat a tablespoon of oil in a frying pan. Add a bowlful of small bread cubes. Sprinkle with dried basil and/or fresh, minced garlic (or dried granulated garlic). Stir-fry over medium high heat until golden brown and crispy.

Dried granulated garlic is great in cooking and better than garlic powder, garlic salt or dried garlic flakes in many recipes.

MEAT, CHICKEN, FISH

Baked Chicken

Prep: 5 minutes. Cook: 2 hours to 2-1/2 hours. 4 servings.

This is the easiest, no-mess, no-basting, hasslefree way to "roast" a chicken. Use leftovers to make Curry Chicken (see below). If you need a lot of leftovers, bake two chickens, same time, same trouble. A "black casserole" (roaster made of porcelain enamel on steel) would be ideal for this dish.

1	Broiler-fryer chicken	1
2 cups	Water	500 mL
2 tbsp	Chicken bouillon liquid concentrate (or microwave 3 bouillon cubes in 3 spoonfuls of water for one minute, stir until smooth)	30 mL
2 tsp	Salt	10 mL

Preheat oven to 350°F (175°C). Wash the chicken and place it in a roasting pan. Pour water in the pan. Brush chicken with bouillon concentrate, and sprinkle with salt. Cover tightly with lid or aluminum foil. Bake for about 2 hours to 2-1/2 hours (depending on size) until nicely browned and tender and the juices run clear when poked with a fork. (If desired, add washed unpeeled potatoes and turnip cut in big chunks, peeled whole onions and carrots halfway through cooking; they cook up juicy and succulent in the broth. Please see page 85 about "black casserole" for baking chicken.)

Curry Chicken

Prep: 10 minutes. Bake: 1 hour (or microwave: 20 minutes). 4 servings.

Divine and easy. Start planning leftover rice and chicken just for this recipe. (Use broccoli instead of zucchini if preferred.)

3 cups	Cooked rice	750 mL
1 cup	Leftover chicken (bite-size)	250 mL
2	Medium zucchini, unpeeled, sliced thinly	2
2 cans	Cream of chicken soup, do not dilute (10 oz. / 284 mL each)	2 cans
4 tbsp	Mayonnaise	60 mL
1 tsp	Dried curry powder	5 mL

Preheat oven to 350°F (175°C). Spread rice in casserole, cover with chicken, then with zucchini slices. In bowl, mix undiluted cream of chicken soup with mayonnaise and curry, and spread it evenly over zucchini. Cover and bake for 1 hour. (Or microwave covered for 20 minutes at 100%; let stand for 5 minutes.)

Baked Fish And Vegetables

Prep: 10 minutes. Bake: 25 minutes (after defrosting). 2 servings.

Use only white and light green parts of leek, sliced, separated into rings, then rinsed well to remove any grit. The basic Béchamel sauce, spiked with pepper and soy sauce and topped with cheese, is so delicious you'll want to eat it right away. If desired, replace leek and zucchini with broccoli and carrot sticks or other veggies, whatever is in season.

1	Leek, sliced into rings, rinsed	1
2	Medium zucchini, unpeeled, thinly sliced	2
1/2 lb	Fresh or frozen fish fillets (defrosted*)	250 g
	Salt and lemon pepper to taste	
2	Tomatoes, sliced	2
3 tbsp	Butter	45 mL
3 tbsp	All-purpose flour	45 mL
1-1/2 cups	Milk	375 mL
1/4 tsp	Black pepper	1 mL
1 tbsp	Soy sauce	15 mL
1/2 cup	Old cheddar cheese, shredded	125 mL
	Herb mixture to taste (such as Mrs. Dash® or Spike®)	

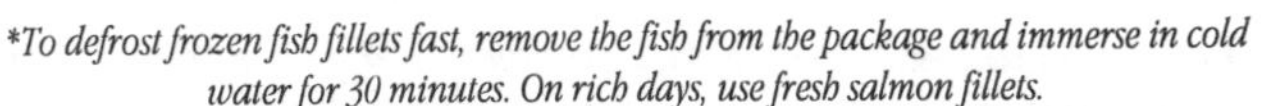

**To defrost frozen fish fillets fast, remove the fish from the package and immerse in cold water for 30 minutes. On rich days, use fresh salmon fillets.*

Preheat oven to 425°F (220°C). Grease an ovenproof casserole. In medium saucepan, bring a cupful of water to a boil with leek and zucchini. Reduce the heat to medium low and simmer, covered, for 5 minutes (do not overcook), drain. Spread fish fillets in casserole, sprinkle a bit of salt and generous dash of lemon pepper all over. Spread partially cooked leek rings and zucchini over fish, top with tomato slices. **To make sauce:** In medium saucepan, melt butter on medium high. Whisk in flour and stir for 1 minute. Whisk in milk, pepper and soy sauce, and stir constantly with wire whisk over medium high heat for 4 minutes until smooth and bubbling. Pour sauce over fish and vegetables. Sprinkle with cheese, and top with dried herbs. Bake uncovered for 25 minutes. Serve with rice or scoop up the sauce with crusty bread.

Lemon pepper is a delicious blend of lemon and coarsely crushed black pepper. Use it for fish, hot cheese sandwiches, dips, salads and soups, and for Divine Dip (page 96).

Chicken Chop Suey

Prep: 15 minutes. Total time: 30 minutes. 4 servings.

Tasty and very easy, requiring just some cutting, slicing and tossing.

2 tbsp	Vegetable oil	30 mL
1	Chicken breast, boneless, cut into tiny strips	1
3	Sliced carrots	3
3	Stalks celery, sliced	3
2 tbsp	Soy sauce	30 mL
2 cubes	Chicken bouillon	2 cubes
1 tsp each	Dried ginger powder and granulated garlic	5 mL each
4 cups	Bean sprouts	1 L

In large frying pan, heat oil at medium high. Stir-fry chicken strips for 2 minutes. Add sliced carrots and celery. Sprinkle with soy sauce, crumbled bouillon cubes, ginger and garlic. Stir-fry for 2 minutes. Spread bean sprouts on top. Reduce heat to medium, cover and simmer for 10 minutes. Turn heat off, toss to mix and let stand for a few minutes.

Roasted Drumsticks

Prep: 10 minutes. Bake: 1 hour. 6-8 servings.

This thick sweet-and-sour sauce, rich in color and flavor, makes chicken succulent and delicious. Very easy to make, cannot fail. Leftovers are tasty cold.

	About 20 drumsticks	
	SAUCE:	
4 tbsp each	Soy sauce and chili sauce	60 mL each
2 tbsp each	Liquid honey, brown sugar, Worchestershire sauce, all-purpose flour	30 mL each
1 tsp each	Dried granulated garlic, onion powder	5 mL each

Preheat oven to 400°F (200°C). Rinse drumsticks and arrange them side-by-side in roasting pan. Mix all sauce ingredients together in measuring cup or small bowl; it yields 1 cup (250 mL) of sauce, enough for about 20 drumsticks (or a pile of wings). Spread sauce all over the chicken. Bake uncovered for 60 minutes.

Navy Bean Stew

Prep: 10 minutes. Cook: 3 hours. 6 servings.

It takes hours to simmer to succulent perfection but requires just minutes of working time. This is especially delicious the next day, so make the whole recipe even if you're only cooking for yourself. Satisfies big hunger.

2 tbsp	Vegetable oil	30 mL
2	Medium onions, chopped	2
1 lb	Stewing beef, cubed bite-size	500 g
3 cubes	Beef bouillon	3 cubes
6 cups	Water	1,5 L
1-1/2 cups	Dried navy beans	375 mL
2 tbsp	Tomato paste	30 mL

In large soup pot, heat oil for 2 minutes at medium high. Add onions and cubed beef, and stir-fry for 5 minutes until lightly browned. Add bouillon cubes, water, beans and tomato paste. Bring to a boil over high. Reduce heat to low, cover and simmer for 3 hours, stirring occasionally. The beans become golden brown and succulent. Serve with rice or use bread chunks to savor the delicious sauce.

MEAT • CHICKEN • FISH

Stovetop Rice And Meat

Prep: 10 minutes. Cook: 20 minutes. 4-6 servings.

An easy one-dish meal.

1 lb	Ground beef	500 g
1 tbsp	HP Sauce	15 mL
1 can	Diced tomatoes (28 oz. / 796 mL), do not drain	1 can
1-1/2 cups	Water	375 mL
1 pouch	Onion soup mix	1 pouch
1 can	Corn (12 oz. / 340 mL)	1 can
1 cup	Long-grain rice, uncooked	250 mL

In large frying pan or saucepan over high heat, stir-fry meat with HP Sauce. Stir in remaining ingredients. Bring to a boil. Turn heat to low, cover and simmer for 20 minutes until rice is fully cooked and all liquid absorbed. Fluff with fork.

TOMATO PASTE: When you need only a spoonful or two of canned tomato paste, spoon the leftovers into a self-sealing freezer bag and press flat to spread it into a thin layer. Freeze, then break off a piece as needed in recipes.

KIELBASA CASSEROLE

Prep: 10 minutes. Bake: 1-1/2 hours. 4 generous servings.

Satisfies big hunger and tastes like grandma's old-fashioned comfort food. Just minutes to put together, it takes time to bake but is worth the wait. When it's ready, turn the heat off but leave the casserole in the oven; it stays warm for an hour or more and gets even more succulent.

1 lb	Kielbasa (Polish sausage) or smoked bratwurst or knockwurst or ham	500 g
4	Medium potatoes	4
2 each	Carrots, medium onions	2 each
1 can	Green beans, drained 14 oz. / 400 mL	1 can
1 can	Cream of celery, 10 oz. / 284 mL	1 can
1/2 can	Milk (use soup can to measure)	1/2 can
	Black pepper to taste	

Preheat oven to 350°F (175°C). Use a large ovenproof casserole with lid. Put all ingredients in it as soon as they are prepared. Pull the casing off sausage, cut in bite-size chunks. Scrub potatoes and cube bite-size. Peel carrots & onions, cut in chunks. Add beans, toss to mix. In bowl, whisk milk with soup, season with black pepper and pour all over the ingredients in the casserole. Cover and bake for 1-1/2 hours until potatoes are very tender.

CARIBBEAN RICE & HAM

Prep: 5 minutes. Total time: 25 minutes. 4 servings.

Easy to make in large quantity for a crowd.

2 cups	Water	500 mL
1/2 tsp	Salt	2 mL
1 cup	Uncooked long-grain rice	250 mL
1 cup	Shredded ham	250 mL
1 cup	Shredded cheese (Gruyère or old cheddar)	250 mL
1 can	Pineapple tidbits (14 oz. / 400 mL)	1 can
Pinch	Cayenne pepper	Pinch

In medium saucepan, bring water to a boil. Add salt and rice, stir once. Reduce heat to minimum, cover and simmer for 17 minutes. Uncover and fluff the rice with fork. Stir ham, cheese and pineapple into hot rice, and add some of the pineapple juice. Stir. Sprinkle lightly with cayenne pepper.

CRUNCHY BAKED FISH FILLETS

Total time: 20 minutes (after defrosting). 2 servings.

Crunchy outside, moist and flaky inside. Bakes fast so you will barely have time to throw a salad together before the meal is done. Refrigerate leftovers for tomorrow to make a fish sandwich for lunch with mayonnaise and lettuce.

1/2 lb.	**Fresh or frozen white fish fillets (haddock or sole, defrosted*)**	**250 g**
1 cup	**Corn flakes**	**250 mL**
1	**Large egg**	**1**
1 tsp	**Lemon juice**	**5 mL**
	Salt and lemon pepper to taste	

(To defrost frozen fish fillets fast, remove the fish from the package and immerse in cold water for 30 minutes.)*

Preheat oven to 425°F (220°C). Put corn flakes in a plastic bag and crush with fist to reduce the flakes to coarse crumbs. Line a baking sheet with aluminum foil and grease the foil. In shallow bowl or deep plate, beat egg and lemon juice together with fork. Rinse fish fillets (cut them in half if very large) and pat dry with paper towel. Dip the fillets into the egg mixture, both sides, then press each side in corn flake crumbs. Place the fillets side-by-side on the prepared baking sheet. Sprinkle lightly with salt and lemon pepper. Bake for 10-14 minutes until fish flakes easily when tested with fork. Do not overbake.

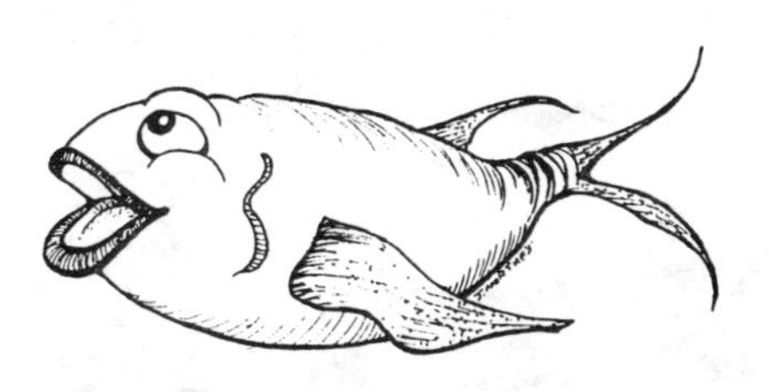

ABSOLUTELY DO NOT MISS: Curry chicken, page 60.

Avoid disappointments; read through the recipe first to see if you have all the ingredients and enough time to make it.

HAMBURGERS

Total time: 15 minutes. Makes 8 hamburgers.

To keep the hamburgers moist and tender, cook them on medium high heat to seal in the juices. Freeze leftover cooked patties. *(See vegetarian burgers on pages 72-73.)*

1 lb	**Ground beef**	**500 g**
	Vegetable oil or butter	
	Salt and black pepper	

You'll also need hamburger buns and your favorite toppings (relish, mayonnaise, ketchup, mustard, HP sauce, shredded lettuce, sliced tomatoes, sliced onions, sliced pickles, sliced cheese, and whatever else you desire)

With moist hands, shape the beef into egg-size balls, then flatten the balls between your hands into thin patties. Arrange the patties on a sheet of waxed paper or a plate. Heat frying pan for 2 minutes over high heat, add a touch of oil or butter and reduce the heat to medium high. Fry the patties until well done and nicely browned on each side, then season with a sprinkle of salt and black pepper. Toast the split buns or heat them in the oven, add burgers and toppings to your taste.

To freeze raw patties, put waxed paper in between each patty for easy separation, put them in a container, cover and freeze. Remove a few patties at a time as needed.

Recycle squeeze-top ketchup and mustard bottles. Clean them well and use for vegetable oil, liquid honey, molasses etc. Try to find a small pump-bottle for cooking oil; it's no-drip and allows you to use drops at a time.

Meat And Macaroni Casserole

Prep: 20 minutes. Bake: 1 hour. 4-6 servings.

Old-fashioned satisfaction. If you like meat and pasta, you'll make this often. Heat leftovers tomorrow in the microwave or stir-fry them on the stovetop.

4 cups	Water	1 L
1 tsp	Salt	5 mL
2 cups	Macaroni (small elbows)	500 mL
1 lb	Ground beef	500 g
2	Medium onions, chopped	2
2	Large eggs	2
2 cups	Milk	500 mL
	Salt, black and white pepper to taste	

Preheat oven to 400°F (200°C). Grease a large ovenproof casserole (8 cups or 2 L). Put water and salt in large saucepan, cover and bring to full boil. Add macaroni, stir once (reduce the heat a bit if necessary to prevent boiling over), and cook uncovered for 10 minutes; drain and pour into the prepared casserole. Meanwhile, in large frying pan, brown ground beef and onions over high heat, stirring frequently, for 8 minutes. Season with salt and black pepper to your taste. Pour meat on pasta and stir to mix. In medium bowl, whisk eggs with milk, season with salt and white pepper, and pour mixture over macaroni and meat. Cover and bake for 40 minutes. Remove the cover and continue baking for another 20 minutes so top becomes crisp and brown.

MEAT/CHICKEN/FISH RECIPES IN OTHER CATEGORIES:

- **Seafood chowder (57)**
- **Chicken soup (58)**
- **Italian spaghetti sauce (85)**
- **Meatballs (86)**
- **Chili con carne (87)**
- **Chinese chicken and vegetables (89)**

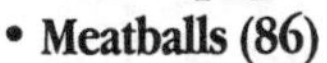

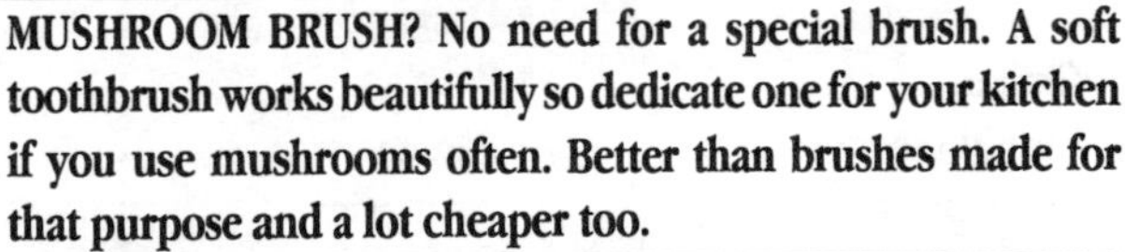

MUSHROOM BRUSH? No need for a special brush. A soft toothbrush works beautifully so dedicate one for your kitchen if you use mushrooms often. Better than brushes made for that purpose and a lot cheaper too.

SCRUBBING POTATOES? The best bet is a very stiff nailbrush with a handle so you'll get a good grip. Works for celery and other stuff too. Better than brushes made for that purpose.

Senegalese Peanut Sauce & Chicken

Total time: 30 minutes. 4-6 servings.

Serve it with fresh bread, plain rice and steamed green vegetables (okra, broccoli, zucchini, green pepper) to savor the delicious sauce.

4 tbsp	Vegetable oil	60 mL
4	Large onions, thinly sliced	4
1 lb	Chicken pieces (wings, sliced drumsticks "osso pollo", boneless breast, bite-sized, or other pieces)	500 g
1 tbsp	Grated fresh gingerroot	15 mL
1 can	Tomato paste (5-1/2 oz. or 156 mL)	1 can
3 cups	Water	750 mL
4 tbsp	Peanut butter	60 mL
	Cayenne pepper, chili powder (or Tabasco sauce), and salt to taste	

Heat oil in large frying pan or soup pot, add onions, cover and cook over medium high heat for 5 minutes, stirring frequently. Add chicken pieces, cover and cook for 5-7 minutes until browned, turning them over once or twice. Add remaining ingredients, stir, cover and cook over medium high heat for 10 minutes.

Delicious vegetarian variation: Instead of chicken, use eggplant, cut into sticks and stir-fried in oil until browned. Season with salt and put aside while you do the rest. Then add eggplant to the sauce.

DRIED HERBS AND SPICES USED IN THIS BOOK:

- Basil
- Black pepper
- Cayenne pepper
- Chili powder
- Cinnamon
- Cumin powder
- Curry powder
- Ginger
- Granulated garlic
- Lemon pepper
- Mustard powder
- Onion powder
- Oregano
- Paprika
- Parsley
- Turmeric
- White pepper
- Herb mixture*

*such as Mrs. Dash® or Spike®

VEGETARIAN

MASHED POTATOES

Prep: 8 minutes. Cook: 15-20 minutes. 2-4 servings.

6	Medium potatoes, peeled, cubed bite-size (3 cups or 750 mL)	6
1/2 cup	Water	125 mL
1/2 tsp	Salt	2 mL
3 tbsp	Butter	45 mL
1/2 cup	Milk	125 mL

In medium saucepan, uncovered, bring potatoes, water and salt to full boil, (watch it so it won't boil over). Reduce heat to medium low, cover tightly, and simmer for 15-20 minutes until very tender (test with fork). Do not drain; there should be hardly any liquid left at this point. Turn heat off. Add butter and milk, stir for a minute so the milk gets warm, then use a masher (or wire whisk or fork) to beat the potatoes until fluffy and smooth; add a little more milk if too thick. If desired, stir in grated cheese and chopped green onions.

Potato patties: *Make patties from cold leftovers. Press both sides into crushed cornflakes or breadcrumbs, and bake for 20 minutes at 350°F (175°C).*

VEGETARIAN

BAKED RICE PILAF

Prep: 10 minutes. Bake: 30 minutes. 4 servings.

Fragrant aroma will permeate your apartment while this pilaf is baking. (Freeze extra portions in self-sealing bags and defrost in microwave oven. Double or triple the recipe so you'll have extra for lunches, add some stir-fried vegetables and canned beans with pasta sauce, topped with grated cheese, and heat in microwave oven.)

3 tbsp	Butter	45 mL
3	Garlic cloves, grated	3
1	Large onion, chopped	1
1 cup	Basmati or long-grain rice, uncooked	250 mL
2 cubes	Vegetable bouillon	2 cubes
2 cups	Hot water	500 mL
	Grated Parmesan cheese	

Preheat oven to 400°F (200°C). In saucepan, melt butter over medium high heat. Add garlic, onion and dry, uncooked rice. Stir-fry for 4 minutes until rice is translucent. Put the rice into an ovenproof casserole. Dissolve bouillon cubes in hot water and pour over rice. Stir well. Cover tightly and bake for 30 minutes. (Stir in some grated Parmesan cheese if desired.)

RICH RICE

Prep: 3 minutes. Total time: 20 minutes. 4 servings.

2 cups	Water	500 mL
1 cup	Converted rice, uncooked (such as Uncle Ben's)	250 mL
4 tsp each	Soy sauce, vegetable oil, butter, and vegetable bouillon concentrate (or microwave 2 bouillon cubes in 2 spoonfuls of water for 30 seconds, stir until smooth)	20 mL each
	Herb mixture (Mrs. Dash® or Spike®)	

In medium saucepan, bring water to a boil. Add rice, stir once. Reduce heat to minimum, cover tightly and simmer for 17-20 minutes. Stir remaining ingredients into hot rice. (Variation: Add a can of corn and chopped green onions and heat through.)

VEGETARIAN

BAKED POTATO SKINS

Prep: 10 minutes. Total time: 45 minutes. 2-4 servings.

4	Large potatoes	4
2 tbsp	Vegetable oil	30 mL
2 tbsp	Vegetable bouillon liquid concentrate (or microwave 3 bouillon cubes in 3 spoonfuls of water for one minute, stir until smooth)	30 mL
	Herb mixture (Mrs. Dash® or Spike®)	
	Black pepper and paprika to taste	
	Grated Parmesan cheese	
	(Optional: Simulated bacon bits)	

Preheat oven to 400°F (200°C). Grease baking sheet, set aside. Choose beautiful, clean potatoes, scrub them very well and cut lengthwise into four pieces. With knife, cut out most of the flesh from each section, leaving thick skins. (Use removed flesh to make mashed potatoes; see recipe on page 70.) Put skins in medium saucepan and add 1/2 cup (125 mL) water. Bring to a boil, reduce the heat, cover and simmer for 5 minutes until medium tender (do not overcook), drain. In small bowl, mix oil with bouillon liquid concentrate, season to taste. Put potato skins, cut sides up, side-by-side, on prepared baking sheet. Brush with prepared oil-bouillon mixture. Sprinkle with Parmesan cheese. Bake for 20-30 minutes until tender and crisp. (Variation: When ready, top skins with mashed potatoes and bacon bits before serving.)

CHINESE FRIED RICE

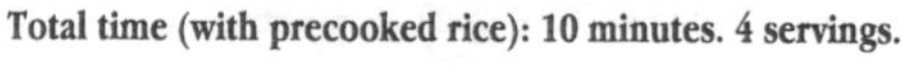

Total time (with precooked rice): 10 minutes. 4 servings.

3 tbsp	Vegetable oil	45 mL
3 cups	Cooked rice (chilled)	750 mL
1	Medium onion, chopped	1
1 tbsp	Grated fresh ginger	15 mL
2 each	Celery stalks & zucchini, diced	2 each
1 cup	Frozen green peas	250 mL
2	Large eggs	2
3 tbsp	Soy sauce	45 mL
	Salt and black pepper to taste	

(To cook rice, see page 35.) Heat oil in frying pan. Add cold rice, onion, ginger, celery, zucchini & peas, and stir-fry over medium high heat for 6 minutes. In small bowl, beat eggs and soy sauce together with fork, sprinkle over rice. Keep stir-frying for a few minutes until eggs are set. Season with salt and pepper.

SESAME OAT VEGGIE BURGERS

Total time: 25 minutes. Makes 8 patties.

Tasty and satisfying alternative to hamburgers. Eat hot or cold with buns and all your favorite "hamburger" fixings. Save a few for tomorrow's brown-bag lunch. When you have a hamburger party for friends (see meat version on page 66), make some of these burgers for vegetarian friends and everyone can share the fixings and buns; also see next recipe.

1 cup	Rolled oats	250 mL
1	Medium onion, chopped	1
1 cup	Shredded cheese (cheddar, mozzarella, or Monterey Jack)	250 mL
1/4 cup	Sesame seeds	60 mL
1/2 tsp	Dried granulated garlic	2 mL
2 tbsp	Soy sauce	30 mL
2	Large eggs	2
	Vegetable oil for frying	

In large bowl, stir together all ingredients. Moisten your hands with water and form the mixture into 8 balls. Heat oil in frying pan over medium high heat, enough to lightly coat bottom. Four at a time, put balls into hot frying pan; immediately flatten each ball with wet spatula into patties (they are fragile at this point so do not disturb them while they are cooking). Fry for 3 minutes on each side until crisp and brown.

Bean Tofu Burgers

Total time: 25 minutes. Makes 12 patties.

Another nutritious, inexpensive and very filling burger idea. Eat hot or cold with some sauce (like HP or BBQ). Great for brown-bag lunch. Can be frozen. (Use leftover or frozen, cooked rice. Cooking rice: Page 36.)

1/2 lb	Firm tofu	250 g
1 cup	Canned red kidney beans (about 1/2 can), drained	250 mL
1 tbsp	Vegetable bouillon liquid concentrate (see recipe below)	15 mL
2 tbsp	Soy sauce	30 mL
2	Large eggs	2
1 cup	Cooked rice, chilled	250 mL
1 cup	Breadcrumbs	250 mL
	Vegetable oil for frying	

With fork, crumble tofu and crush beans on a large plate. (Do not purée them in blender.) In large bowl, stir together all ingredients. Between your wet hands, press the mixture into 12 patties. In frying pan over medium high heat, heat enough oil to lightly coat bottom. Six at a time, fry patties for 4 minutes on each side until crisp and brown.

VEGETARIAN

Zucchini Sticks

Prep: 10 minutes. Bake: 30 minutes. 4 servings.

Great snack hot or at room temperature. Zucchini must be fresh and firm.

4	Medium zucchini	4
1 tbsp	Vegetable oil	15 mL
4 tsp	Vegetable bouillon liquid concentrate (or microwave 2 bouillon cubes in 2 spoonfuls of water for 30 seconds, stir until smooth)	20 mL
	Dried granulated garlic	
	Grated Parmesan cheese & breadcrumbs	

Preheat oven to 400°F (200°C). Cut washed, unpeeled zucchini into small finger-size sticks, then arrange them side-by-side (not on top of each other) on nonstick baking sheet, cut side up. In small bowl, stir together oil and bouillon concentrate, brush over zucchini sticks with pastry brush. Sprinkle granulated garlic and grated Parmesan cheese all over, top very lightly with breadcrumbs. Bake for 30 minutes until tender crisp. Tasty hot or cold.

Creamy Corn Casserole

Prep: 10 minutes. Cook: 10 minutes plus bake: 30 minutes. 2 servings.

4 cups	Water	1 L
1 tsp	Salt	5 mL
2 cups	Elbow macaroni, uncooked	500 mL
4 tbsp	Melted butter	60 mL
1 can	Creamed corn (12 oz. - 340 mL)	1 can
1 can	Corn, do not drain (12 oz. - 340 mL)	1 can
1 cup	Diced cheese (cheddar or Velveeta)	250 mL
1	Medium onion, chopped	1

VEGETARIAN

Preheat oven to 350°F (175°C). In large saucepan, bring water and salt to a boil. Add macaroni (reduce the heat a bit if necessary to prevent boiling over), cook for 10 minutes, drain. Mix all ingredients in ovenproof casserole. Bake for 30 minutes, uncovered. (Or microwave 10 minutes on high, stirring occasionally.)

Baked Ziti

Prep: 5 minutes. Total time: 45 minutes. 2 servings.

One of the easiest, tastiest and cheapest Italian recipes around that everybody loves. Prepared pasta sauce in a jar or can is cheap and good. Double or triple the recipe for a crowd. Great also the next day heated in microwave or on stovetop. (If you want a meat version, just add some browned ground beef before baking ziti in the oven.)

1 cup	Elbow macaroni, uncooked	250 m
1-1/2 cups	Pasta sauce	375 mL
1	Medium onion, chopped	1
3/4 cup	Mozzarella cheese, grated	180 mL
4 tbsp	Grated Parmesan cheese	60 mL
4 tbsp	Breadcrumbs	60 mL

Preheat oven to 350°F (175°C). In large saucepan, cook macaroni in boiling water for 10 minutes, drain. Put cooked macaroni into a small, shallow baking dish (cake pan works well, about 9" or 23 cm square). Spread pasta sauce, onion and mozzarella on top and stir to mix. Sprinkle with Parmesan cheese and breadcrumbs. Bake for 30 minutes, uncovered, until hot and bubbling.

ROASTED VEGETABLES

Prep: 10 minutes. Cook/bake: 40 minutes. 2 hungry or 4 polite servings.

Quantities and ingredients are flexible. Boiling the vegetables partially cuts down the baking time. Leftovers are excellent heated in a microwave oven.

1 cup	**Water**	**250 mL**
2 tbsp	**Butter**	**30 mL**
1 cube	**Vegetable bouillon**	**1 cube**
3 each	**Potatoes, zucchini, celery sticks, carrots, all cut bite-size**	**3 each**
4	**Medium onions, peeled, quartered**	**4**
2 cups	**Fresh whole mushrooms**	**500 mL**
	Herb mixture (Mrs. Dash® or Spike®)	

Preheat oven to 375°F (190°C). In frying pan or large saucepan, bring to a boil water, butter and bouillon cube. Add all vegetables except mushrooms, reduce the heat to medium, cover and simmer for 8 minutes; do not overcook. Put everything, including mushrooms and any remaining liquid, into a roasting pan. Sprinkle herb mixture on top. Bake uncovered for 30 minutes.

VEGETARIAN

GLAZED CARROTS

Total time: 17 minutes. 2-4 servings.

Carrots are delicious. Buy a big bag and use for Sunshine Salad, Colorful Coleslaw For One, Carrot Pineapple Muffins, carrot sticks for crunching raw, and for this easy caramelized side dish.

1/2 cup	**Water**	**125 mL**
6	**Medium carrots, peeled and cut into small sticks**	**6**
2	**Medium onions, peeled, sliced**	**2**
2 tbsp	**Butter**	**30 mL**
3 tbsp	**Brown sugar**	**45 mL**
1 tsp	**Dried ginger**	**5 mL**
2 tbsp	**Lemon juice**	**30 mL**

In frying pan, bring water to a boil. Add carrots and onions, cover and cook over medium high heat for 7 minutes until tender crisp and all the water has been absorbed. Add butter and sugar, sprinkle with ginger and lemon juice, and stir-fry for 3 minutes.

ABSOLUTELY DO NOT MISS: Spinach mini-quiches, page 90.

Macaroni And Cheese Casserole

Prep: 15 minutes. Total time: 1 hour. 4 servings.

Old-fashioned comfort food. The sauce is so good that if your hunger or schedule doesn't allow waiting, skip the baking and just eat the sauce with cooked macaroni.

4 cups	Water	1 L
1 tsp	Salt	5 mL
2 cups	Elbow macaroni, uncooked	500 mL
2 tbsp	Butter	30 mL
1	Large onion, chopped	1
4 tbsp	All-purpose flour	60 mL
2 cups	Milk	500 mL
1 cup	Shredded cheese (mozzarella, Monterey Jack or cheddar)	250 mL
	Salt and black pepper to taste	
4 tbsp	Breadcrumbs	60 mL
4 tbsp	Grated Parmesan cheese	60 mL

Preheat oven to 375°F (190°C). Grease ovenproof casserole. In large saucepan, bring water to full boil. Add salt and macaroni (stir once and reduce the heat a bit if necessary to prevent boiling over) and cook for 10 minutes, drain. Meanwhile, in medium saucepan, melt butter. Add onion and flour, and stir-fry for 2 minutes over medium high heat with a wire whisk. Whisk in milk. Stirring constantly over medium high heat, bring to a boil and cook for about 4 minutes until sauce thickens. Remove from heat. Add cheese and season with salt and pepper, stir with wire whisk until smooth. Spread cooked macaroni in prepared casserole. Stir in the sauce. Sprinkle breadcrumbs and Parmesan cheese on top. Bake uncovered for 45 minutes.

Tofu Sandwich

Total time: 6 minutes.

Cut slices of firm tofu (approximately 1/4" or 6 mm thick). Brush a little oil in frying pan, heat and add tofu slices. Sprinkle with a few drops of vegetable bouillon concentrate (to substitute, see page 57), lemon pepper and dried herb mixture. Fry both sides briefly over medium high heat. Great hot or cold. Makes a tasty sandwich filler; add a dab of mustard, lettuce and sliced tomato.

Potato Frittata

Prep: 10 minutes. Cook: 15 minutes. 2 hungry or 4 polite servings.

This is one large pancake, easy to make even for beginners. Leftovers are tasty cold and make a good lunch for tomorrow.

3	**Large potatoes, peeled, grated**	**3**
1	**Large onion, chopped**	**1**
2	**Large eggs**	**2**
3 tbsp	**All-purpose flour**	**45 mL**
1/2 tsp	**Salt**	**2 mL**
1/4 tsp	**Black pepper**	**1 mL**
	Vegetable oil for frying	

In medium bowl, stir together all ingredients except oil. Heat two tablespoons of oil in large nonstick frying pan over medium high heat for 3 minutes. Spread all the mixture evenly in hot pan. Lower the heat slightly, cover and cook for 7-8 minutes until bottom is golden brown and top almost set. Loosen with spatula and slide frittata onto a flat plate. Flip the plate quickly upside down over the frying pan (hold onto frittata edges with your fingers) so frittata lands in the pan browned side up. Cook, uncovered, for 6-7 minutes. Slide onto large plate and cut into wedges. Eat with apple sauce, sour cream or ketchup.

VEGETARIAN

Variation (small latkes): Heat oil in large frying pan over medium high heat. Drop large spoonfuls of mixture into hot oil, fry each side for 3 minutes.

Broccoli Potatoes

Prep: 10 minutes. Cook: 15 minutes. 2 servings.

This dish looks delicious and tastes even better than mashed potatoes.

1 cup	**Water**	**250 mL**
4	**Large potatoes, peeled, cut bite-size**	**4**
1 bunch	**Broccoli, cut bite-size**	**1 bunch**
2 tbsp	**Butter**	**30 mL**
4 tbsp	**Cream cheese**	**60 mL**
Dash	**Salt**	**Dash**

In large saucepan, bring to a boil water, potatoes and broccoli. Reduce heat to low, cover and simmer for 15 minutes until very tender. Uncover, continue cooking until all the water has evaporated. Turn heat off. Add butter and cream cheese in small pieces, sprinkle with salt, and stir gently so butter and cheese melt but potatoes remain partly chunky. Do not overmix and do not mash.

Tofu Risotto

Prep: 15 minutes. Total time: 60 minutes. 4-6 servings.

Don't be discouraged by the long list of ingredients. This dish is a snap.

2 tbsp	Vegetable oil	30 mL
1 lb	Firm tofu, diced	500 g
1	Green pepper, chopped	1
1	Medium onion, chopped	1
4 tbsp	Soy sauce	60 mL
1 cup	Long grain rice, uncooked	250 mL
1 cup	Chopped parsley	250 mL
3	Celery stalks, sliced	3
2	Carrots, sliced	2
1/2 cup	Shredded cheese (cheddar)	125 mL
1 tbsp	Grated fresh gingerroot	15 mL
2 cups	Hot water	500 mL
2 cubes	Vegetable bouillon	2 cubes

Preheat oven to 400°F (200°C). Heat oil in frying pan over medium high heat for 2 minutes. Add tofu, green pepper and onion, sprinkle soy sauce on top, and stir-fry for 5 minutes until tofu turns golden. In ovenproof casserole, mix remaining ingredients and stir in tofu mixture. Cover tightly and bake for 45 minutes until rice is fully cooked and all the liquid has been absorbed.

Creamy Pasta Veggie Combo

Prep: 10 minutes. Total time: 20 minutes. 4 servings.

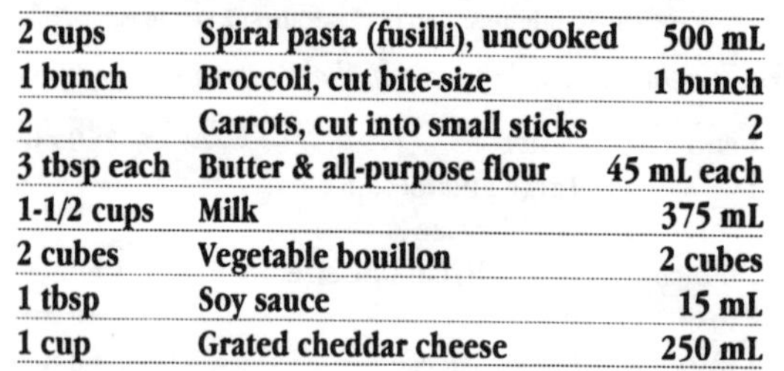

2 cups	Spiral pasta (fusilli), uncooked	500 mL
1 bunch	Broccoli, cut bite-size	1 bunch
2	Carrots, cut into small sticks	2
3 tbsp each	Butter & all-purpose flour	45 mL each
1-1/2 cups	Milk	375 mL
2 cubes	Vegetable bouillon	2 cubes
1 tbsp	Soy sauce	15 mL
1 cup	Grated cheddar cheese	250 mL

In soup pot, bring to a boil 8 cups (2 L) of water. Add pasta, broccoli and carrots, and cook uncovered for 10 minutes. Drain, return to the pot. Meanwhile, in medium saucepan, melt butter, add flour and stir for 1 minute with wire whisk. Add milk, bouillon cubes and soy sauce. Bring to a boil, stirring constantly. Lower heat to medium high and stir with whisk for 4 minutes. Add cheese and stir until velvety smooth. Pour sauce over hot pasta & veggies, and toss to mix.

Tofu Fricassée

Total time: 10 minutes. 2 servings.

1 tbsp	Vegetable oil	15 mL
1/2 lb.	Firm tofu, diced	250 g
1	Tomato, diced	1
2 tsp	Vegetable bouillon concentrate (or microwave 1 bouillon cube in spoonful of water for 30 seconds, stir until smooth)	10 mL
	Lemon pepper & herb mixture to taste	

Heat oil in frying pan over medium high heat. Add tofu and tomato, sprinkle with liquid bouillon concentrate, lemon pepper and dried herb mixture. Stir-fry for 7 minutes until golden brown. Eat with rice and salad, or use as a filler in pita pocket, tacos or in bean burritos. (See page 81 about tofu.)

VEGETARIAN

Hummus

Total time 8 minutes. Makes 2 cups (500 mL).

Hummus, an increasingly popular mid-Eastern chick pea purée, is very easy to make. You'll find tahini (sesame seed paste) in health food stores; store it tightly covered in refrigerator. Store prepared hummus in closed container in refrigerator; it keeps for several days. Use it as a dip and sandwich spread.

1 can	Chickpeas (about 2 cups or 500 mL)	1 can
4 tbsp	Tahini paste	60 mL
2-3	Garlic cloves, grated	2-3
1/2 tsp	Salt	2 mL
2 tbsp	Lemon juice	30 mL
1 tbsp	Dried parsley	15 mL
1 tsp	Dried cumin powder	5 mL
1/4 cup	Water	60 mL

Rinse and drain chickpeas. If you have a food processor, put all the ingredients in and blend until smooth. (If it is too thick, add a bit more water.) Or, crush chickpeas with fork until smooth, add the remaining ingredients and mix well. Great with pita bread and as a dip for tortilla chips and baguette bits with friends. For authentic serving, spread some hummus on a plate, pour a little olive oil on top and decorate with chopped fresh parsley; serve with pita.

Don't miss other great dips & chips: pages 95-96.

Ratatouille

Prep: 15 minutes. Total time: 40 minutes. 4 servings.

This French vegetable stew is great hot or cold. Use leftovers for hot cheese sandwiches, pita melts or submarines, or as a filler with cheese for crêpes. Or spread leftovers over rice or pasta, top with grated cheese and bake in microwave or regular oven. Choose a shiny, firm, unbruised, fresh and young eggplant so it's almost seedless and not bitter.

1/3 cup	**Vegetable oil, divided**	**75 mL**
1	**Small eggplant, unpeeled, cubed bite-size**	**1**
2	**Small zucchini, sliced**	**2**
1	**Large onion, sliced**	**1**
1	**Green pepper, cut bite-size**	**1**
6	**Garlic cloves, chopped**	**6**
3	**Ripe red tomatoes, skinned*, chopped**	**3**
	Salt, pepper, dried oregano and basil to taste	

** See below for how to skin tomatoes.*

VEGETARIAN

Heat half of the oil in large frying pan. Add eggplant cubes to hot pan and stir-fry over medium high heat for 5 minutes until lightly browned. Set aside in a large saucepan. Add a bit more oil to frying pan and stir-fry zucchini for 3 minutes; transfer to saucepan. Add remaining oil to frying pan, stir-fry onion and green pepper for 3 minutes; transfer to saucepan. Add garlic, tomatoes, salt, pepper, oregano and basil to saucepan. Heat the saucepan over medium high heat until the stew starts bubbling. Reduce the heat, cover and simmer for 15 minutes. Remove cover and continue simmering for 5-10 minutes until most of the liquid is gone. Serve with rice.

GARLIC: Freeze whole garlic cloves, unpeeled; then peel & grate frozen cloves as needed. Easy & practical. Grating is better than chopping and releases more flavor.

GRATER: The good old-fashioned 4-sided metal grater still works well. One side with small upward holes grates garlic cloves like a charm (frozen garlic cloves grate especially well).

To skin tomatoes for cooking or baking, cover them with boiling water, let stand for one minute and pull the skin off.

TROPICAL BEANS  

Total time: 15 minutes. Serves 4.

This easy and fast, one-dish complete meal is satisfying and tasty. Keep some leftovers for tomorrow's lunch. Reheating intensifies flavors.

2 tbsp	Vegetable oil	30 mL
1	Chopped onion	1
1 tsp	Dried granulated garlic	5 mL
1 tbsp	Grated fresh gingerroot	15 mL
2 cups	Cooked rice, chilled	500 mL
1 can	Black beans*, drained (about 19 oz. or 540 mL)	1 can
2 tbsp	Soy sauce	30 mL
4 tsp	Vegetable bouillon liquid concentrate (or microwave 2 bouillon cubes in 2 spoonfuls of water for 30 seconds, stir until smooth)	20 mL
1 can	Pineapple tidbits (14 oz. / 398 mL)	1 can

** Or red or pinto or romano beans*

Heat oil in large frying pan over medium high heat. Add onion and garlic, and stir-fry for 3 minutes until golden brown. Add gingerroot and rice, stir-fry for 3 minutes. Add beans, drizzle soy sauce and vegetable bouillon all over, top with pineapple, and stir-fry for 5 minutes to heat and blend flavors.

TOFU: Tofu (bean curd) is made from soy milk which is coagulated and pressed into blocks. Recipes in this book call for firm tofu, available in oriental food stores, most supermarkets, and health food stores. Cholesterol-free and low in saturated fats, tofu is a very healthy, inexpensive non-animal source of protein, calcium, iron and minerals. Bland on its own, it easily absorbs seasonings and romances beautifully with lemon pepper, paprika, bouillon cubes or liquid concentrate, soy sauce and herbs. Check the expiration date on the package. Sniff it before using; fresh tofu has no smell, rancid tofu has an offensive odor. Once removed from the package, immerse unused portions in cold water, cover and refrigerate for up to seven days (change water every two days). You can use tofu instead of meat, chicken or fish in most recipes, particularly in stews and casseroles, and in stir-fried recipes.

• Bean tofu burgers (73) • Tofu, veggies & couscous (89)
• Tofu risotto (78) • Tofu sandwich (76) • Tofu fricassée (79)

Zucchini Fritters (or Frittata)

Total time: 25 minutes. Makes 12 fritters or 1 large frittata.

These are good hot or cold. Very little oil will be absorbed if the oil is hot enough to seal the surface of fritters or frittata. Stash extra fritters into a pita pocket for lunch to go. Use a splatter guard so the oil won't splash all over the place. A slotted spoon is handy to turn fritters over.

2	Large eggs	2
1/2 tsp	Salt	2 mL
Dash	Black pepper	Dash
3	Medium zucchini, unpeeled, grated (about 3 cups or 750 mL)	3
1	Medium carrot, grated	1
1	Medium onion, chopped	1
1/2 cup	All-purpose flour	125 mL
	Vegetable oil for frying	

VEGETARIAN

In large bowl, using a fork, beat eggs with salt and pepper. Add zucchini, carrot and onion. Sprinkle flour on top, stir until well blended.

FRITTERS: In frying pan, heat enough oil to generously coat the bottom. Drop heaping tablespoons of batter into hot oil, flatten and cook over medium high heat until golden brown and crisp around edges, about 3-4 minutes on each side. Drain on paper towels.

FRITTATA: Heat 2 tbsp (30 mL) of oil in frying pan (brush it around to cover the entire bottom). Spread the mixture in hot frying pan. Reduce heat to medium, cover and cook for about 4-6 minutes until golden brown underneath. Use a spatula to loosen the frittata and slide it onto a flat plate uncooked side up. Flip the plate quickly upside down over the frying pan (hold onto frittata edges with your fingers) so the frittata lands in the frying pan browned side up. Cook, uncovered, for 4 minutes or so. Cut into wedges.

ABSOLUTELY DO NOT MISS:
Roasted vegetables, page 75.
Cream of mushroom soup, page 55.
Chinese chicken and vegetables, page 89.
Crunchy granola cakes, page 98.
Oat flatbread, page 104.
Baked pancake, page 113.

Crowd Pleasers

Stuffed Mini-Pitas

Mini-pitas, white or whole-wheat, are inexpensive and just the right size to make little sandwiches for a party. Available in packages of about 16, they make ideal finger-food since the pita opens up into a small edible pocket to hide all sorts of delicious surprises. You can make a whole pile in advance; some are great cold while others can be heated at the last minute. To heat, wrap prepared mini-pitas in aluminum foil (or arrange in roasting pan and cover), bake in hot oven for 15 minutes. Refrigerate others. Make several fillings to suit different tastes: vegetarian, meat, spicy, mild.

Several ideas for fillings are shown here to get you started:

Cooked rice & beans (crushed with fork), pasta sauce, grated cheese. Heat.	Canned tuna or salmon, mayonnaise, chopped celery & onion. Eat cold.	Browned ground beef & onions, BBQ or HP Sauce, rice or veggies. Heat.
Pepperoni slices, pasta sauce, grated cheese. Heat.	Stir-fried chopped vegetables, a little blue cheese. Heat.	Chopped spinach, ricotta, feta cheese, garlic. Heat.
Chopped hard-boiled eggs, a few drops of oil, salt & pepper. Eat cold.	Hummus (page 79), a slice of tomato, fresh parsley or dill. Eat cold.	Stir-fry onions, sliced mushrooms, herbs & tomatoes in a little oil. Eat hot or cold.

CROWD

ABSOLUTELY DO NOT MISS THE FOLLOWING CROWD PLEASERS IN OTHER CATEGORIES:

- Tortilla pizzas (38)
- Rich nachos (38)
- Bean burritos (39)
- Gourmet melt (42)
- Melba melts (43)
- Hot Russian sandwich (41)
- Coleslaw (47)
- Bean salad (47)
- Greek salad (49)
- French onion soup (54)
- Curry chicken (60)
- Roasted drumsticks (62)
- Hamburgers (66)
- Veggie burgers (72-73)
- Baking (98-108)
- Sweet stuff, beverages (110-117)

Italian Spaghetti Sauce

Prep: 15 minutes. Cook: 3 hours. 8 servings.

This takes only a few minutes of working time but hours to cook to perfection, so plan accordingly. However, it simmers without any work on your part so it's well worth the wait. When the sauce is ready, then and only then cook the spaghetti. See page 33 for cooking pasta. If you have leftover sauce, you can freeze some, use some for lasagna, as a "Sloppy Joe" for pitas, or simply reheat with some leftover pasta or rice.

2 tbsp	Vegetable oil	30 mL
8	Garlic cloves, minced	8
1	Large onion, chopped	1
1 lb.	Ground beef	500 g
1 can	Diced tomatoes (28 oz. / 796 mL)	1 can
1 can each	Tomato soup, sliced mushrooms (10 oz. / 284 mL)	1 can each
1 can	Tomato paste (5-1/2 oz. or 150 mL)	1 can
2 each	Carrots, celery stalks, sliced	2 each
2 tsp each	Salt and oregano	10 ml each
1/2 tsp	Black pepper	2 mL
Pinch	Chili powder	Pinch

Variation: Add diced pepperoni to sauce for more flavor.
Vegetarian variation: Omit ground beef.

In large soup pot, heat oil, add garlic and onion and sauté for 5 minutes over medium high heat. Add meat and stir-fry, breaking into pieces, until browned. Add remaining ingredients, bring to a boil, then reduce heat to minimum, cover and simmer for 3 hours, stirring once in a while.

"Black casserole" (oval roaster with cover, made of porcelain enamel on steel) is inexpensive, lightweight, and simply marvelous for baking chicken, and for all sorts of casseroles and roasts for a crowd. Cleans easily too.

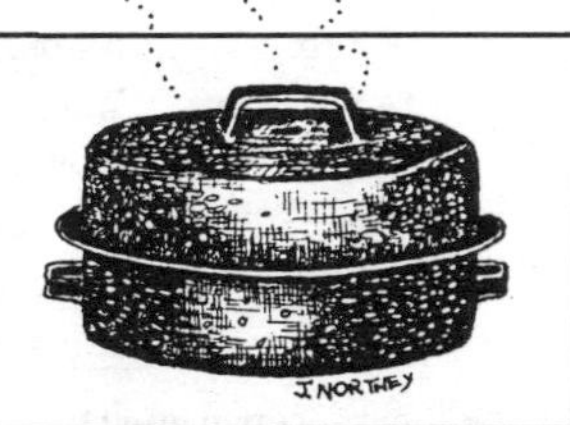

Keep some butter in a covered dish at room temperature for easy spreading. You'll use less too.

CROWD

MEATBALLS

Total time: 25 minutes. Makes 36 meatballs.

Mama's old-fashioned comfort food with a contemporary touch. Double or triple the recipe as needed. Add potatoes, rice or pasta and gravy (below).

1/3 cup	Water	75 mL
1 tsp	Salt	5 mL
1/2 tsp	Black pepper	2 mL
2 tbsp	Dried parsley	30 mL
1/3 cup	Breadcrumbs	75 mL
1	Large onion, chopped	1
1	Large egg	1
1 lb	Ground beef	500 g
	Vegetable oil for frying	

In large bowl, mix water with salt, pepper and parsley. Add remaining ingredients and mix well. With moist hands, roll the mixture into walnut-size balls & put them on a wet plate. Oil the frying pan very lightly and heat at high for 2 minutes. Add meatballs, cover and fry over medium high heat for 8 minutes until well cooked and browned on each side. Shake the pan several times to brown the balls evenly and retain their round shape. Or bake the balls in preheated oven (375°F or 190°C) for 20 minutes on a greased baking sheet.

CROWD

BROWN GRAVY

Total time: 10 minutes. Makes 1-1/2 cups (375 mL).

This basic gravy goes well with meatballs and potatoes. Make a satisfying mini-meal by mixing leftovers with croutons (page 58) and cubed cheese, then heat the combo and spoon it up. (See Poutine, page 92.)

2 tbsp	Butter	30 mL
2 tbsp	All-purpose flour	30 mL
1-1/2 cups	Water	375 mL
1 cube	Beef bouillon (or chicken or vegetable bouillon)	1 cube
1/2 tsp	Worchestershire sauce	2 mL
	Salt and black pepper to taste	

In medium saucepan, melt butter over high heat. Add flour and stir for 1 minute with wire whisk. Whisk in water, bouillon cube and Worchestershire sauce. Bring to a boil, then cook over medium heat, whisking frequently, for 5 minutes until thick and smooth. Taste and lightly season with salt and pepper. (Optional: Stir-fry one sliced onion in the butter before adding flour.)

Chili Con Carne

Prep: 15 minutes. Total time: 30 minutes. 6-8 servings.

Always popular for a hungry crowd. Get a loaf of crusty bread to accompany this meal.

2 tbsp	**Vegetable oil**	**30 mL**
2	**Medium onions, chopped**	**2**
1 lb	**Ground beef**	**500 g**
2-4 tsp	**Chili powder**	**10-20 mL**
1/2 tsp	**Dried cumin powder**	**2 mL**
1 can	**Diced tomatoes (28 oz. / 796 mL)**	**1 can**
2 tbsp	**Tomato paste**	**30 mL**
1 cup	**Water**	**250 mL**
1 cube	**Beef bouillon**	**1 cube**
1	**Can red kidney beans (19 oz. / 540 mL), do not drain**	**1**
1	**Can white kidney beans (19 oz. / 540 mL), do not drain**	**1**

In soup pot, heat oil at medium high heat. Add onions and beef and stir-fry until browned, for about 7 minutes. Add remaining ingredients. Bring to a boil, reduce the heat, cover and simmer for 15 minutes. (Check the taste and add extra chili powder if needed.)

CROWD

If you accidentally pour too much salt or pepper into soup or other liquid, DO NOT STIR. Immediately pour the food into another casserole; chances are that the salt or pepper has become a lump or fallen to the bottom and can be removed.

ABSOLUTELY DO NOT MISS:
Scalloped potatoes for one, page 41.
Pasta frittata, page 43.
Tropical beans, page 81.

TACOS

Prep: 15 minutes.

Make some with meat, others with vegetarian filling. Better yet, organize all fillings on separate plates and let everyone make their own version.

You'll need taco shells plus fillings of your choice

Meat filling: Taco packages have instructions. Basically, you'll brown some ground beef, add the seasoning mix that comes in the package plus some water and simmer until liquid has evaporated. If you buy taco shells without seasoning mix, just add some pasta sauce when you brown the ground beef, then season with salt, pepper and a splash of Worchestershire sauce or Tabasco. Heat taco shells in the oven for a few minutes. Fill with browned meat, lettuce, tomatoes, shredded cheese and taco sauce. If you want softer tacos, fill with cooked meat before heating the shells.

Vegetarian filling: Instead of meat, fill tacos with cooked or canned beans (heat the beans first) and/or Tofu Fricassée (see page 79). Drizzle bottled steak sauce (such as HP) on beans. Top with shredded lettuce, chopped cucumbers, tomatoes, plus shredded carrots and cheese. Add some taco sauce or salsa on top.

BROCCOLI CHEESE SQUARES

Prep: 10 minutes. Bake: 1 hour. Makes 25 small squares.

Equally good warm or at room temperature.

4	**Large eggs**	**4**
1/2 cup	**All-purpose flour**	**125 mL**
1 bunch	**Chopped broccoli, uncooked (about 3 cups / 750 mL)**	**1 bunch**
1	**Large onion, chopped**	**1**
2 cups	**Cottage cheese**	**500 mL**
1 cup	**Grated cheese (old cheddar)**	**250 mL**
1/2 tsp each	**Salt and black pepper**	**2 mL each**

Preheat oven to 400°F (200°C). Grease or spray a cake pan (9" or 23 cm square). Whisk eggs with flour until smooth. Stir in remaining ingredients. Spread into prepared cake pan. Bake for 1 hour. Let cool for at least 15 minutes and cut into squares.

Store mushrooms in brown paper bag in the refrigerator to keep them fresh. Eat within a few days.

Chinese Chicken And Vegetables

Prep: 15 minutes. Cook: 10 minutes. 4-6 servings.

The rich, thick sauce is finger-licking good. The list of ingredients is long but this dish is very easy and fast to make.

2 tbsp	Vegetable oil	30 mL
2	Boneless chicken breasts, cut into small strips	2
2	Medium onions, sliced	2
2	Carrots, cut into tiny sticks	2
3	Celery stalks, sliced	3
1 bunch	Broccoli, cut bite-size	1 bunch
1	Red pepper, sliced thinly	1
2 tbsp	Grated fresh gingerroot	30 mL
1-1/2 cups	Water	375 mL
3 cubes	Chicken bouillon	3 cubes
3 tbsp	Cornstarch	45 mL
2 tbsp	Brown sugar	30 mL
4 tbsp	Soy sauce	60 mL
2 tbsp	Lemon juice	30 mL

Vegetarian variation: Use diced tofu instead of chicken and vegetable bouillon instead of chicken bouillon.

CROWD

Heat oil in large frying pan or soup pot. Add chicken strips and stir-fry over medium high heat for 3 minutes until nicely browned. Add onions, carrots, celery, broccoli and pepper, and stir-fry for 2 minutes. In bowl, mix all remaining ingredients, pour over chicken & veggies. Bring to a boil, stirring constantly, until sauce thickens. Reduce the heat to medium low, cover and simmer for 10 minutes. Serve with rice or couscous (see below).

Tofu, Veggies & Couscous

Prep: 15 minutes. (Quantities and ingredients are flexible.)

Heat a little oil in frying pan over medium high heat. Add diced tofu (see page 81 about tofu) and stir-fry for a few minutes until nicely browned. Add colorful raw vegetables such as broccoli pieces, carrots sticks, red and yellow pepper slices, snow peas, and mushrooms. Sprinkle with Hoisin Sauce and a tiny bit of Ground Hot Chili Garlic Sauce (both available at oriental food stores), and stir-fry for 5 minutes. Meanwhile, put 1 cup (250 mL) of couscous in a bowl, add two tablespoons of oil and 1 cup (250 mL) of boiling water. Stir, cover and let stand for 3 minutes. Serve couscous on a plate and arrange veggies on top.

Spinach Mini-Quiches

Prep: 10 minutes. Bake: 35 minutes. Makes 12 mini-quiches.

Eat warm or cold. Each mini-quiche looks delicious and won't fall apart.

1 tbsp	Vegetable oil	15 mL
1	Medium onion, chopped	1
1 tsp	Dried granulated garlic	5 mL
1	Package frozen chopped spinach (about 1-1/2 cups or 375 mL), defrosted and drained*	1
3	Large eggs	3
4 tbsp	All-purpose flour	60 mL
1 cup	Cottage cheese	250 mL
1 cup	Shredded cheese (old cheddar)	250 mL
1/2 tsp	Salt	2 mL

Preheat oven to 400°F (200°C). Lightly grease or spray 12 large muffin cups. Heat oil in frying pan at medium high, add onion and sauté for 3 minutes. Remove onion to a large bowl, stir in remaining ingredients. Divide the mixture into prepared muffin cups. Bake for 35 minutes until golden brown. Let cool for at least 15 minutes. (*See next page on how to defrost spinach.)

Variation: Add chopped ham and/or crumbled feta cheese.

CROWD

Vegetarian Chili

Prep: 10 minutes. Total time: 25 minutes. 6-8 servings.

4 tbsp	Vegetable oil	60 mL
2	Large onions, chopped	2
2 tsp	Chili powder (or to taste)	10 mL
	Salt and black pepper to taste	
1 tbsp	Dried granulated garlic	15 mL
2 cans	Diced tomatoes, undrained (19 oz. / 540 mL each)	2 cans
2 cans	Corn, do not drain (12 oz. / 340 mL each)	2 cans
1/2 cup	Tomato paste	125 mL
2 cans	Red kidney beans, do not drain (19 oz. / 540 mL each)	2 cans
2 cups	Water	250 mL

Heat oil in soup pot at medium high, add onion & stir-fry for 3 minutes. Stir in remaining ingredients and bring to a boil. Reduce heat and simmer, uncovered, for 15 minutes. Serve with fresh bread or rice.

Russian Quiche

Prep: 20 minutes. Bake: 10 minutes & 40 minutes. 4 servings.

At its best warm or at room temperature. Surprisingly easy and so delicious that it might soon become one of your favorites. Makes a perfect late-night snack for friends. Save leftovers for tomorrow's lunch.

	CRUST:	
1 cup	**All-purpose flour**	**250 mL**
1/4 tsp	**Salt**	**1 mL**
4 tbsp	**Butter, softened**	**60 mL**
4 tbsp	**Ice cold water**	**60 mL**
	FILLING:	
2	**Large eggs**	**2**
3/4 cup	**Light cream (or half-and-half)**	**180 mL**
Pinch each	**Black and white pepper**	**Pinch each**
3/4 cup	**Shredded cheese (old cheddar)**	**180 mL**
3/4 cup	**Cooked ham, chopped**	**180 mL**
1 pkg.	**Frozen chopped spinach (about 1-1/2 cups or 375 mL), defrosted and drained***	**1 pkg.**

Preheat oven to 425°F (220°C). Grease a pie plate. In bowl, mix flour, salt and butter with your fingers, add water and mix into smooth dough. Press dough into prepared pie plate (line bottom and edges), prick with fork all over, and bake for 10 minutes. Meanwhile, whisk together eggs and cream. Season with pepper. Stir in cheese, ham and spinach. Spread the mixture on the prepared pie shell. Bake for 40 minutes. Let cool for at least 20 minutes. Cut into wedges.

***TO DEFROST FROZEN SPINACH:** Remove package. Put frozen spinach on microwavable plate. Microwave at full blast for 5 minutes. Remove from oven, put another plate on top, bottom down, with defrosted spinach in the middle. Press plates tightly together over sink to squeeze out excess liquid.

If you do not have a microwave oven, defrost the spinach in a saucepan on the stovetop in a little water at medium high heat. Drain.

If you prefer using fresh spinach, remove stems, wash the leaves well and chop.

POUTINE

Total time: 10 minutes.

(Pronounced Poo'**tin**.*) This is Quebec's contribution to the world of comfort & "junk" food. Heat canned gravy or make your own as shown below.*

Frozen French fries (from a bag)
Cheese (cheese curds or cubed mozzarella)
Optional: Cooked sausage, pepperoni, or fried onions

	BROWN GRAVY:	
2 tbsp	Butter	30 mL
2 tbsp	All-purpose flour	30 mL
1-1/2 cups	Water	375 mL
1 cube	Beef bouillon	1 cube
1/2 tsp	Worchestershire sauce	2 mL

Bake French fries in the oven on baking sheet as shown on the package. Meanwhile, make the gravy. In medium saucepan, melt butter on high. Whisk in flour and stir for 1 minute. Whisk in remaining ingredients. Bring to a boil, then cook over medium heat, whisking frequently, for 5 minutes until smooth. (Taste & season with salt & pepper.) Makes 1-1/2 cups (375 mL). To serve poutine, put two handfuls of hot French fries in a bowl, add a handful of cheese (curds or cubed) on top and pour some hot gravy all over.

BÉCHAMEL SAUCE

Total time: 7 minutes. Makes 1 cup (250 mL).

Béchamel, the basic white sauce, is great as a lasagna topping, for potatoes and cooked pasta. It can be embellished with cheese and herbs for any occasion. Mix some crushed, hard-boiled eggs with Béchamel and eat with boiled or baked potatoes. Spread some on steamed vegetables, add sliced mozzarella cheese on top and bake in hot oven until cheese melts and bubbles. This sauce over stir-fried vegetables also makes an excellent filler for crêpes.

2 tbsp	Butter	30 mL
2 tbsp	All-purpose flour	30 mL
1 cup	Milk	250 mL
	Salt and white or black pepper to taste	

In medium saucepan, melt butter over medium high heat. Add flour and stir with wire whisk for 1 minute. Whisk in the milk, bring to a boil, and cook over medium high heat for 4 minutes until thick and velvety smooth, stirring constantly with wire whisk. Season lightly with salt and pepper.

VEGETARIAN LASAGNA 

Prep: 30 minutes. Bake: 60 minutes. 4 hungry or 8 polite servings.

Few things are as popular and satisfying as lasagna. This one is so rich and delicious that you won't miss the meat. It is time-consuming, especially the first time around (messy too, with several dishes to wash), but well worth the trouble of learning to make it. It's a recipe you'll make again and again. Leftovers taste great reheated in a microwave oven (cover first to keep your oven clean). Freeze leftovers for hungry days. Save some for tomorrow's lunch.

20	**Lasagna noodles (one package)**	**20**
2 tbsp	**Vegetable oil**	**30 mL**
4 cups	**Raw vegetables (chopped onion, diced green pepper, sliced zucchini and mushrooms)**	**1 L**
3 cups	**Pasta sauce (1 jar)**	**750 mL**
1 pkg.	**Chopped frozen spinach (about 1-1/2 cups or 375 mL), defrosted & drained (see page 91)**	**1 pkg.**
2 cups	**Cottage cheese**	**500 mL**
2	**Large eggs**	**2**
1 tbsp	**Dried basil**	**1 tbsp**
1/2 tsp	**Salt**	**2 mL**
1 cup	**Béchamel sauce (see recipe on previous page)**	**250 mL**
	Sliced mozzarella cheese	

Meat version: *Just mix browned ground beef with vegetables and pasta sauce.*

In large soup pot, cook noodles according to package directions. (**I like oven-ready noodles, but I cook them for 3-4 minutes** to make them pliable and moist; they never stick together.) Pour out most of the hot water, then fill the pot with cold water so the lasagna won't be too hot to handle and won't stick together. Meanwhile, in large frying pan, heat oil, add diced, raw vegetables and stir-fry at medium high for 15 minutes. Add pasta sauce, cover and cook at medium high for 10 minutes. In large bowl, stir together defrosted spinach, cottage cheese, eggs, basil and salt. Preheat oven to 350°F (175°C). Spread half of the prepared vegetable-pasta sauce in lasagna pan (or roasting pan). Spread 5 noodles on top, side-by-side, overlapping partly if necessary. Spread remaining sauce on top and add 5 more noodles. Spread half of the spinach mixture on top, add 5 noodles, then the remaining spinach mixture. Top with remaining noodles. Spread the prepared Béchamel sauce all over and cover with sliced cheese. Bake for 60 minutes, uncovered, until golden brown.

PIZZA

Prep: 30 minutes. Rising: 60 minutes. Bake: 12-14 minutes. Makes one large rectangular pizza (11" x 17" or 28 cm x 43 cm baking sheet), or four small round pizzas.

If you wish to make a pizza from scratch, you'll be surprised how easy and fun it is once you master it. If you make individual pizzas (8-10 small round ones or by dividing a large rectangular one into smaller sections before adding toppings), everybody can dress up their pizza to their taste.

	DOUGH:	
1 tsp	**Sugar**	**5 mL**
1 cup	**Lukewarm water**	**250 mL**
1 envelope	**Active dry yeast (traditional, not quick rise)**	**1 envelope**
1 tsp	**Salt**	**5 mL**
3 tbsp	**Vegetable oil**	**45 mL**
2-1/2 cups	**All-purpose flour**	**625 mL**
	SAUCE:	
1/2 cup	**Canned or bottled pizza sauce**	**125 mL**

TOPPINGS: Let your imagination go wild with toppings. Anything goes. A few possibilities: Green & red peppers, sliced onions and tomatoes, olives, garlic, mushrooms, capers, shredded ham or pepperoni or cooked bacon, shrimp, pineapple, oil-marinated sun-dried tomatoes, fresh spinach, anchovy fillets. Oregano, basil, garlic.

Shredded mozzarella on top

In large bowl, stir sugar in lukewarm water. Sprinkle in yeast, let stand for 10 minutes, then stir to blend. Stir in salt and oil. Add all but a handful of the flour. (Use remaining flour for tabletop and kneading.) Lightly flour clean tabletop, turn dough out onto it. Lightly sprinkle flour on top, knead for 5 minutes until it's smooth and elastic and no longer sticks to hands (sprinkle with little flour on top as needed). Shape the dough into a ball, oil surface lightly and place in bowl, cover. Let stand on tabletop in warm place away from drafts until doubled in size, about 1 hour. Preheat oven to 500°F (260°C). Grease one rectangular baking sheet (or four aluminum pie plates). Roll out the dough to fit the sheet or pie plates. Your hands are the best "rolling pins" to rotate, press and stretch the dough until thin enough, or use a bottle as a rolling pin. Spread a thin layer of pizza sauce on dough, dress with toppings of your choice, add shredded mozzarella on top. Bake on a lower rack for crusty bottom for 12-14 minutes until crust is golden and cheese is bubbly.

Dips And Chips  

Everyone loves dips and spreads with chips, crackers, raw vegetables (carrots, celery, broccoli, cucumber, red/green peppers, cauliflower, young zucchini).

❍ **TORTILLA CHIPS:** Lightly brush flour tortillas (or split pita bread) with vegetable oil. Cut into eight triangular wedges and arrange side-by-side on a baking sheet. Bake for 6-8 minutes at 300°F (150°C) until crisp. (Optional: Before cutting and baking, sprinkle the tortillas very lightly with Parmesan cheese and some spices such as lemon pepper, chili or cayenne pepper, sweet red paprika, onion powder, dried granulated garlic or garlic salt.)

❍ **LOW-FAT OR FAT-FREE CHIPS:** Cut flour tortillas or split pita bread halves into triangles and bake for 6-8 minutes at 300°F (150°C) until crisp.

❍ **BAGUETTE BITS:** Thinly slice day-old baguette. Arrange slices side-by-side on a baking sheet. Bake for 15 minutes at 350°F (175°C) until dry and crisp. Store dried slices in covered container.

❍ **GARLIC BREAD:** Use a baguette, a loaf of French or Italian bread, or buns (white or whole wheat), cut lengthwise in half or sliced, or pita bread. Brush the cut surface lightly with oil or melted butter, sprinkle with fresh, grated (or dried, granulated) garlic and bake for 5 minutes at 350°F (175°C) until crusty and fragrant. Serve immediately. (Sprinkle with dried basil, marjoram, thyme, parsley, or paprika and Parmesan cheese, in addition to garlic, if desired.)

❍ **BAGEL BITS:** This is a perfect way to preserve bagels before they get bad (whole-wheat/raisin, white, multigrain or other flavors). Cut the bagel into small disks (slicing all around the bagel, makes about 16-20 per bagel), or quarter each sliced half of a bagel. Arrange the pieces side-by-side on a large plate and let dry at room temperature until hard. Or arrange the pieces on a baking sheet and bake for 12-15 minutes at 300°F (150°C) until dry and crisp. Store dried bagel bits in a plastic bag or covered container. Great with cream cheese, dips and soups anytime. Make a big pile for a party.

❍ **SALSA:** Excellent varieties are available commercially but it's easy to make your own fresh version. Just mix together finely chopped ingredients: fresh tomatoes, red raw onions, celery, jalapeño peppers, garlic cloves and green pepper. Season with lemon juice, basil, salt and black pepper to taste. (Add chopped fresh cilantro, i.e. coriander leaves, if available.) Chill. Make salsa a few hours in advance so flavors will blend to perfection. It keeps for several days in refrigerator.

❍ **SAVORY MAYO:** Mix 1/2 cup (125 mL) of mayonnaise with a tablespoon each of ketchup and HP or BBQ Sauce.

❍ **DIVINE DIP:** Roast one whole head of garlic (8-10 cloves; do not peel or separate) at 375°F (190°C) for 40 minutes. Squeeze cloves to remove soft, roasted flesh. Mix with a small package of cream cheese. Add lemon pepper.

❍ **FETA DIP:** Mix equal parts of crumbled feta cheese, ricotta and plain yogurt. Add a little lemon juice, grated garlic clove and fresh, chopped parsley.

❍ **EGG DIP:** Crush four peeled hard-boiled eggs with a fork, stir with 4 tbsp (60 mL) of mayonnaise. Season with salt and pepper. (If desired, add chopped fresh dill or parsley or green onions.)

❍ **BLUE CREAM CHEESE DIP:** Mix equal parts of softened cream cheese, plain yogurt, and crumbled blue cheese. Add a touch of Dijon mustard and fresh or dried herbs of your choice.

❍ **SOUR CREAM & ONION DIP:** This old favorite is still popular. Mix 2 cups (500 mL) of sour cream with one pouch of dry onion soup mix.

❍ **SALMON DIP:** Mix one can of salmon, 4 tbsp (60 mL) mayonnaise, touch of lemon juice. Optional: Add finely chopped celery and/or red onion. Stir vigorously until smooth. (When available, add lots of chopped fresh dill.)

❍ **GUACAMOLE:** When avocado yields to gentle pressure, it's ready. (Ripen a hard avocado faster by placing it in a brown paper bag at room temperature.) Slit avocado in half and remove the pit. Scoop out flesh onto large plate and crush coarsely with fork (do not mash or purée). Sprinkle with lemon juice, add chopped tomato & onion (and, if desired, some minced green pepper or jalapeño, minced garlic or coriander). Stir and season with salt and pepper. (To keep leftover guacamole green, cover dish with plastic wrap, pressed onto the surface to remove air and refrigerate; use within 24 hours.) **Ripe avocado can be frozen (unpeeled), then used later for guacamole.**

❍ **TZATZIKI:** Finely chop one small cucumber, peeled and seeded. Add 1/2 cup (125 mL) each of plain, firm-style yogurt and sour cream, 3 grated garlic cloves, 1/4 tsp (1 mL) of Dijon mustard, sprinkle of lemon juice and a pinch of salt and black pepper.

❍ **HUMMUS:** This popular mid-Eastern chickpea purée makes an excellent dip or spread. See recipe on page 79.

❍ **BEAN SPREAD:** Filling, nutritious, delicious & very easy. See page 39.

Baking Breads, Muffins, Cakes And Cookies

Cheese Biscuits

Prep: 15 minutes. Cook: 15 minutes. Makes 12 biscuits.

You need a clean working surface since you will be kneading the dough. Even if you have never kneaded before, it is easy and takes just minutes.

1	Large egg	1
1/2 cup	Sour cream	125 mL
1/2 cup	Milk	125 mL
2 cups	All-purpose flour	500 mL
1/2 tsp	Salt	2 mL
1 tsp	Dry mustard powder	5 mL
2 tsp	Baking powder	10 mL
1 cup	Shredded cheese (cheddar)	250 mL
1	Medium onion, chopped	1

Preheat oven to 450°F (230°C). Grease a baking sheet or muffin tin or spray it with no-stick cooking spray. In large bowl, whisk together egg, sour cream and milk. Add remaining ingredients, blend well. Turn dough onto floured surface, knead lightly for 3 minutes, sprinkling some flour on top so it won't stick to hands. Roll into thick rope, divide into 12 rolls. Pressing the palm of your hand against a roll, rotating gently, shape it into a round biscuit. Place biscuits on baking sheet or in muffin cups. Bake for 15 minutes until lightly browned and fluffy. Eat warm.

BAKING

Crunchy Granola Cakes

Prep: 10 minutes. Bake: 20 minutes. Makes 12 mini-cakes.

Fast and easy, sweet and satisfying. They keep well and make filling breakfast or snack.

3	Large eggs	3
1/2 cup	Brown sugar	125 mL
1/3 cup	Vegetable oil	75 mL
3 cups	Rolled oats	750 mL
3/4 cup	Raisins (or dried apricots*)	180 mL

**Soak apricots first in hot water for 2 minutes to soften them, rinse well to remove any dirt, then cut in small pieces with kitchen scissors or sharp knife and a cutting board.*

Preheat oven to 350°F (175°C). Grease or spray 12 large muffin cups or line them with paper cups. In large bowl, whisk together eggs, sugar and oil for 2 minutes. Add rolled oats and raisins and stir to mix. Spoon into prepared muffin cups. Bake for 20 minutes.

Carrot Pineapple Muffins

Prep: 10 minutes. Bake: 30 minutes. Makes 12 large muffins.

Be patient and let these cool before eating. They are even better the next day. Moist, sweet, delicious.

1 cup	All-purpose flour	250 mL
1/2 cup	Whole-wheat flour	125 mL
3/4 cup	Brown sugar (packed)	180 mL
2 tsp	Baking powder	10 mL
1 tsp	Cinnamon	5 mL
1/2 cup	Vegetable oil	125 mL
1/2 cup	Orange juice	125 mL
2	Large eggs	2
1 cup	Grated carrots (2 medium)	250 mL
3/4 cup	Crushed pineapple, from can, do not drain	180 mL

Preheat oven to 400°F (200°C). Grease or spray 12 large muffin cups or line them with paper cups. In large bowl, stir together dry ingredients. Add oil, orange juice, eggs, grated carrots and pineapple. Mix until moistened. With large spoon, scoop batter into prepared muffin cups. Bake for 30 minutes. Let them cool in muffin cups for a while before removing.

Note: The batter is so soft that it's practical to put it into a pitcher or large measuring cup and pour into muffin cups with the aid of a spoon. Or use a small ladle to fill the muffin cups.

BAKING

Blueberry Muffins

Prep: 10 minutes. Bake: 25 minutes. Makes 12 muffins.

These are so moist and flavorful that it's hard to believe there is no butter. Eat warm or at room temperature.

1/4 cup	**Vegetable oil**	**50 mL**
1/2 cup	**Orange juice**	**125 mL**
1/2 cup	**Brown sugar**	**125 mL**
2	**Large eggs**	**2**
3/4 cup	**Plain yogurt**	**180 mL**
3/4 cup	**Whole-wheat flour**	**180 mL**
1 cup	**All-purpose flour**	**250 mL**
1 tbsp	**Baking powder**	**15 mL**
2 cups	**Unsweetened blueberries (fresh or frozen; do not defrost)**	**500 mL**

Preheat oven to 400°F (200°C). Grease 12 large muffin cups or line them with paper cups. In large bowl, combine oil, orange juice, brown sugar, eggs and yogurt. Whisk until well blended. Add whole-wheat flour and mix. In another bowl, mix baking powder with all-purpose flour, then toss blueberries in it to coat and add to oil and egg mixture. Stir gently, do not overmix. Spoon the batter into prepared muffin cups. Bake for 25 minutes until golden brown and a toothpick inserted into center comes out dry.

The batter looks purple before baking. Don't worry about it; the baked muffins will be deliciously golden brown.

BAKING

Banana Muffins

Prep: 10 minutes. Cook: 20 minutes. Makes 12 large muffins.

Moist and flavorful, these muffins make good use of overripe bananas. Carry a couple with you for a quick lunch. They do not crumble all over the place. (Freeze overripe, mashed bananas in a plastic bag, tightly closed, and use later for this recipe.)

2	Large eggs	2
1/2 cup	Butter, softened* (salted)	125 mL
2 tsp	Lemon juice	10 mL
1/2 cup	Milk	125 mL
2	Ripe bananas, peeled and mashed with fork	2
1-1/2 cups	All-purpose flour	375 mL
3/4 cup	Brown sugar	180 mL
1 tsp	Baking soda	5 mL
	(Optional: Chopped nuts, seeds or raisins, or chocolate chips)	

**To soften 1/2 cup (125 mL) of butter, microwave it for 1 minute at 30% power. If you use unsalted butter, add a pinch of salt.*

Preheat oven to 350°F (175°C). Grease or spray 12 large muffin cups or line them with paper cups. In large bowl, whisk together eggs, softened butter, lemon juice and milk for 2 minutes. Stir in mashed bananas. In another bowl, mix flour, sugar and soda. Combine the dry mixture with egg mixture and stir with wire whisk until moistened. (Add two handfuls of chopped nuts, or seeds, raisins or chocolate chips if desired.) Put the mixture into a large measuring cup (4 cups or 1 L) or pitcher, and pour into prepared muffin cups, about 3/4 full. Bake for 20 minutes or until toothpick inserted in center comes out dry. (If you use a loaf pan or square cake pan instead of muffin cups, bake for 50-60 minutes.)

BROWN SUGAR GOT HARD? Keep it soft (and make rock-hard sugar soft again overnight) by keeping a slice of fresh bread in your sugar container; close tightly.

Bran Oat Muffins

Prep: 10 minutes. Bake: 25 minutes. Makes 12 large muffins.

2	Large eggs	2
1/4 cup	Vegetable oil	60 mL
1 cup	Unsweetened apple sauce	250 mL
3/4 cup	Brown sugar	180 mL
1 cup	All-Bran	250 mL
1/2 cup	Rolled oats	125 mL
1 cup	All-purpose flour	250 mL
2 tsp each	Baking powder & cinnamon	10 mL each
1 cup	Raisins (or chopped dried fruits)	250 mL

Preheat oven to 375°F (190°C). Spray 12 large muffin cups with no-stick cooking spray or line them with paper cups. In large bowl, using fork or wire whisk, beat eggs with oil, apple sauce and sugar for 2 minutes. Stir in remaining ingredients. Spoon mixture into muffin cups. Bake for 25 minutes until golden brown.

Mocha Squares

Prep: 10 minutes. Bake: 20 minutes. Makes 35 squares.

2	Large eggs	2
1 cup	Sugar	250 mL
1/2 cup each	Milk and melted butter*	125 mL each
1-1/2 cups	All-purpose flour	375 mL
2 tsp each	Baking powder and vanilla	10 mL each
1 tbsp	Cocoa powder	15 mL
	ICING:	
4 tbsp each	Hot water, melted butter*	60 mL each
2 tsp each	Instant coffee granules, vanilla extract	10 mL each
1 tbsp	Cocoa powder	15 mL
1-1/2 cups	Icing sugar (confectioners' sugar)	375 mL
	Shredded coconut for top	

**Use unsalted butter or hard margarine.*

Grease baking pan (9" x 13" x 2" or 23 cm x 33 cm x 5 cm). Preheat oven to 350°F (175°C). In large bowl, whisk eggs and sugar for 2 minutes. Add remaining ingredients, stir until smooth. Spread batter in prepared pan and bake for 20 minutes. Meanwhile, in bowl, stir icing ingredients together until smooth. Leave cake in the pan and spread icing on the hot cake. Let cool for 5 minutes, then sprinkle with shredded coconut. Let cool. Cut into small squares.

BAKING

CHOCOLATE CHEESECAKE

Prep: 15 minutes. Bake: 55 minutes. Makes one 9" (23 cm) cheesecake.

Be patient and let this delicious cheesecake cool completely before devouring it. To hasten the cooling, refrigerate it.

	CRUST:	
1 cup	**Graham crumbs**	**250 mL**
2 tbsp	**Sugar**	**30 mL**
3 tbsp	**Melted butter**	**45 mL**
	FILLING:	
1/2 cup	**Semisweet chocolate chips**	**125 mL**
4 tbsp	**Sugar**	**125 mL**
2 tbsp	**Water**	**30 mL**
8 oz.	**Cream cheese, softened***	**250 g**
1/2 cup	**Sugar**	**125 mL**
1/2 cup	**Sour cream**	**125 mL**
1 tsp	**Vanilla extract**	**5 mL**
2	**Large eggs**	**2**

** Soften cream cheese by taking it out of refrigerator for several hours. Or put it in a microwavable bowl and microwave at medium heat (50%) for 2 minutes.*

Preheat oven to 325°F (160°C). **Crust:** In small bowl, stir graham crumbs with sugar and butter. Spread mixture into pie plate, 9" (23 cm), pat firmly with back of spoon, set aside. **Filling:** In small measuring cup, combine chocolate chips, sugar and water; microwave for 3 minutes at 50% (medium heat) until chocolate melts, stir until smooth; set aside. (Or use a saucepan on stovetop over very low heat.) In large bowl, beat together softened cream cheese, sugar, sour cream and vanilla (wire whisk works well). Add eggs and beat well. Divide batter in half. Stir melted chocolate mixture into first half, and pour this mixture into crumb-lined pan. Cover with plain batter. Marbleize the top with spoon tip by scooping delicately beneath the plain batter to bring swirls of chocolate batter onto the surface for a beautiful design; do not disturb graham mixture. Bake for 55 minutes. Cool at room temperature, then refrigerate. Cut slices cleanly with knife dipped in very hot water.

Variation: Use fresh or frozen strawberries or raspberries instead of chocolate chips/sugar/water combination. If you use a square cake pan instead of a pie plate, cut cheesecake into squares.

ABSOLUTELY DO NOT MISS:
Recipe list for perishables (pages 22-24).

BAKING

Oat Flatbread

Prep: 5 minutes. Bake: 22 minutes. Makes 4 small breads.

Buttermilk is skim milk with bacterial culture, slightly sour, very thick, tasty and healthy. In Scandinavian countries, folks drink it as is. It is great for muffins, wholegrain pancakes, dips, salad dressings and for this super-easy Finnish flatbread. The flatbread keeps well at room temperature and makes a good breakfast or lunch, warm or cold. Be sure to shake the buttermilk before using it so it's thick and smooth. (Flatbread is low-fat if you do not add egg butter on top).

1 cup	**Buttermilk**	**250 mL**
1/4 tsp	**Salt**	**1 mL**
1-1/2 cups	**Rolled oats**	**375 mL**
	EGG BUTTER: **Hard-boiled eggs, softened butter, salt and pepper to taste**	

Preheat oven to 400°F (200°C). Grease baking sheet. In small bowl or large measuring cup, stir salt into buttermilk, add oats and mix. Divide mixture into four heaps on baking sheet, flatten with spoon into round flatbreads. Bake for 22 minutes. **Egg butter:** While the bread is baking, hard-boil 2 eggs. Peel and crush the eggs with a fork, add some butter, season lightly with salt and pepper. Spread over warm flatbread.

Quick Pop-Up Rolls

Prep: 5 minutes. Bake: 18 minutes. Makes 6 rolls.

Make these at the last minute since they are at their best piping hot.

1 cup	**All-purpose flour**	**250 mL**
1 tsp	**Baking powder**	**5 mL**
1/2 tsp	**Salt**	**2 mL**
3 tbsp	**Sugar**	**45 mL**
1/2 cup	**Milk**	**125 mL**
2 tbsp	**Mayonnaise**	**30 mL**

Preheat oven to 375°F (190°C). Grease or spray 6 large muffin cups or line them with paper cups. Stir all ingredients together in a bowl. Fill the prepared muffin cups and bake for 18 minutes. Eat hot with butter or jam.

An empty milk carton makes a great pitcher for crêpe batter; just shake and pour.

CUPCAKES

Prep: 10 minutes. Bake: 20 minutes. Makes 12 large cupcakes.

Easy and deliciously addictive mini-cakes.

3/4 cup	**Sugar**	**180 mL**
1/2 cup	**Butter, softened (unsalted)***	**125 mL**
2	**Large eggs**	**2**
1 tsp	**Vanilla extract**	**5 mL**
3/4 cup	**Milk**	**180 mL**
1-1/2 cups	**All-purpose flour**	**375 mL**
2 tsp	**Baking powder**	**10 mL**
2 tbsp	**Cocoa powder**	**30 mL**

**To soften 1/2 cup (125 mL) of butter, microwave it for 1 minute at 30% power. **If you don't have cocoa powder, use 4 tbsp (60 mL) of chocolate milk mix (such as Quik®).*

Preheat oven to 375°F (190°C). Spray 12 large muffin cups or line them with paper cups. In bowl, beat together sugar, softened butter and eggs with wire whisk for 2 minutes. Stir in vanilla and milk. Sprinkle flour and baking powder on top, and stir with wire whisk until smooth. Fill each muffin cup with 2 tablespoons of batter; you should have about 1/3 of the batter remaining in the bowl. Stir cocoa powder into remaining batter and put about a spoonful into each muffin cup on top of vanilla batter. Bake for 20 minutes.

DATE SQUARES

Prep: 15 minutes. Bake: 30 minutes. Makes 25 squares.

1 cup	**Water**	**250 mL**
2 cups	**Pitted dates (1 package)**	**500 mL**
1-1/2 cups	**All-purpose flour**	**375 mL**
1-1/2 cups	**Rolled oats**	**375 mL**
1/2 cup	**Brown sugar**	**125 mL**
1/2 cup	**Unsalted butter, softened**	**125 mL**

Preheat oven to 375°F (190°C). In medium saucepan, bring to a boil water and dates. Reduce heat to medium low, cover and simmer for 10 minutes until soft. Do not drain; crush with fork and stir until creamy. Grease a cake pan (9" or 23 cm square) and set aside. Meanwhile, in bowl, mix together flour, oats and sugar. With your fingers, mix in butter until it looks like coarse crumbs. Spread half of the crumbs into prepared pan and press flat with back of spoon. Spread the cooked, crushed dates on top. Cover with remaining crumbs and press evenly with back of spoon. Bake for 30 minutes until lightly browned. Let cool before eating. Cut into squares.

Brownies

Prep: 10 minutes. Bake: 25 minutes. Makes 25 squares.

4 tbsp	Unsalted butter	60 mL
2 squares	Unsweetened baker's chocolate	2 squares
2	Large eggs	2
1 cup	Sugar	250 mL
Pinch	Salt	Pinch
1 tsp	Vanilla extract	5 mL
1/2 cup	All-purpose flour	125 mL
1/2 cup	Walnuts, chopped	125 mL
	ICING:	
1 square	Unsweetened baker's chocolate	1 square
2 tbsp	Unsalted butter	30 mL
2 tbsp	Milk	30 mL
1 cup	Icing sugar (confectioners' or powdered sugar)	250 mL

Preheat oven to 350°F (175°C). Grease a cake pan (9" or 23 cm square). In small measuring cup, microwave butter and chocolate for 3 minutes at 50% (medium heat) until chocolate melts; stir until smooth, set aside. (Or use a saucepan on stovetop over very low heat.) In bowl, whisk together eggs, sugar, salt and vanilla until light and fluffy. Stir in chocolate mixture, then flour and walnuts. Spread in prepared pan. Bake for 25-30 minutes. Cool for 10 minutes before spreading icing on top.

ICING: In medium measuring cup, microwave chocolate and butter for 2 minutes at 50% (medium heat) until chocolate melts, stir until smooth. (Or use a saucepan on stovetop over very low heat.) Add milk and icing sugar, stir until smooth. Spread icing on warm cake. Let cool. Cut into squares.

COOKING: Feel free to be creative and improvise.

BAKING: Follow the recipe and measure carefully.

MARGARINE VS. BUTTER: If you use margarine instead of butter for recipes in this book, use hard margarine in a block. Soft, whipped, easy-to-spread margarine in tubs does not work well for cooking or baking.

Chocolate Chip Cookies

Prep: 10 minutes. Bake: 10 minutes. Makes about 36 cookies.

It's soul-satisfying to bake your own cookies from time to time.

1/2 cup	Butter (unsalted), softened*	125 mL
1/2 cup	Granulated sugar	125 mL
1/2 cup	Brown sugar, firmly packed	125 mL
1	Large egg	
1 tsp	Vanilla extract	5 mL
1-1/4 cups	All-purpose flour	300 mL
1 tsp	Baking powder	5 mL
Pinch	Salt	Pinch
1/2 cup	Semisweet chocolate chips	125 mL

Preheat oven to 375°F (190°C). In large bowl, stir together butter and sugars with large spoon. Stir in egg and vanilla, then flour, baking powder and salt. Add chocolate chips and stir to mix (your clean hands work well). Drop small spoonfuls of dough on ungreased cookie sheet about 2" (5 cm) apart. Bake for 10 minutes. Do not overcook; cookies will appear soft, let them cool.

Peanut Butter Cookies

Prep: 15 minutes. Bake: 12 minutes. Makes about 36 cookies.

1/2 cup	Butter (unsalted), softened*	125 mL
1/2 cup	Peanut butter (soft)	125 mL
1/2 cup	Sugar	125 mL
1/2 cup	Brown sugar, firmly packed	125 mL
2	Large eggs	2
1/2 tsp	Vanilla extract	2 mL
1-1/2 cups	All-purpose flour	375 mL
1/2 tsp	Baking soda	2 mL
Pinch	Salt	Pinch

**To soften 1/2 cup (125 mL) of cold butter, microwave it for 1 minute at 30% power.*

Preheat oven to 375°F (190°C). In large bowl, stir together butter, peanut butter and sugars with large spoon. Stir in eggs and vanilla. Combine flour with baking soda and salt, add to mixture and stir to blend. Drop small spoonfuls of dough on ungreased cookie sheet about 2" (5 cm) apart. (If desired, flatten crisscross with fork dipped in flour.) Bake for 12 minutes until lightly browned.

Turn a baking sheet with a rim upside down and it will double as a cookie sheet without a rim.

Chewy Oatmeal Cookies

Prep: 15 minutes. Bake: 10 minutes. Makes about 36 cookies.

1/2 cup	Butter (unsalted), softened*	125 mL
3/4 cup	Packed brown sugar	180 mL
1	Large egg	1
2 tbsp	Cold water	30 mL
1/2 tsp	Vanilla extract	2 mL
3/4 cup	All-purpose flour	180 mL
1/4 tsp	Baking soda	1 mL
Pinch	Salt	Pinch
1-1/4 cups	Rolled oats	300 mL
1/2 cup	Semisweet chocolate chips (or raisins)	125 mL

**To soften 1/2 cup (125 mL) of cold butter, microwave it for 1 minute at 30% power.*

Preheat oven to 350°F (175°C). Stir together butter and sugar with large spoon until creamy. Beat in egg, water and vanilla. Add flour, baking soda, salt and oats and mix well. Stir in chocolate chips (or raisins). Drop small spoonfuls of dough on ungreased cookie sheet about 2" (5 cm) apart. Bake for 10 minutes until edges are golden brown. Cookies appear very soft when hot; do not overbake. Cool completely before storing in covered container.

BAKING

IMPROVISE ON EQUIPMENT: A smooth bottle makes a good rolling pin. Small yogurt containers work well as measuring cups. Use pie plates or foil as a cover. A large, flat plastic plate makes a handy cutting board (liquids won't run overboard). Brand-new, clean, small paint brush is a practical pastry brush.

ABSOLUTELY DO NOT MISS:
Cooking terms: page 11
Conversion table imperial/metric: page 12.
Substitution table: page 13.

Sweet Stuff & Beverages

Sweet Snacks

Moments come when you must have something sweet and fast. Here are a few ideas to caress your taste buds depending on your preference and what's available in your cupboard and refrigerator. Perfect for breakfast too.

Peanut butter and sliced banana on toast. (Add slices of apple, mandarin, raisins, liquid honey.)	**Mix rolled oats (uncooked), raisins, brown sugar, cinnamon, and milk in a bowl.**
In small bowl, put diced apple, raisins, plain yogurt, All-Bran, and brown sugar.	**Cottage cheese plus crushed, canned pineapple (drained) or pineapple chunks.**
Bagel with cream cheese (and perhaps raisins or jam).	**Molasses on hot toast, top with slice of processed cheese.**
Vanilla ice cream with instant coffee powder. Vanilla ice cream with banana & strawberry jam.	**Celery sticks or apple slices with peanut butter or cream cheese.**
Cucumber fruit raita: Stir together chopped cucumber, seedless grapes, drained pineapple tidbits, and plain firm-style yogurt.	**Top hot toast (or sliced & toasted English muffin) with a slice of strong cheddar cheese plus orange marmalade. Great for breakfast.**
Peanut butter and strawberry jam between two pieces of hot toast.	**Microwave a cored apple with maple syrup (or brown sugar and cinnamon) in bowl for 2 minutes.**
Fruit salad: Improvise with whatever fruit you have around; top with plain yogurt, bran, brown sugar (& a touch of ginger).	**Cinnamon toast mix: In covered jar, shake sugar with ground cinnamon (5:1) until blended. Sprinkle on hot buttered toast.**

Baguette cinnamon crisps: Thinly slice day-old baguette. Arrange slices side-by-side on a baking sheet. Lightly brush with melted butter and sprinkle with cinnamon-sugar mix (see above for cinnamon toast mix). Bake for 30 minutes at 300°F (150°C) until dry and crisp.

French Toast   

Total time: about 10 minutes. Makes two French toasts.

A day-old loaf of unsliced French or Italian-style bread (not the ready-sliced kind in a plastic bag) works best, but use whatever you have around. If your bread is too soft and fresh, lightly toast the slices first to create a crisp surface which prevents sogginess.

1	Large egg	1
1/4 cup	Milk	50 mL
2	Thick slices of bread	2
	Butter	
	Cinnamon sugar* and syrup	

little vanilla

*Recipe for cinnamon sugar is on page 110.

Using a fork, beat egg and milk in a shallow bowl. Melt some butter in large frying pan until it sizzles. Dip thick bread slices into the egg mixture on both sides to absorb the liquid, and fry each side over medium high heat until golden brown. Sprinkle cinnamon sugar and syrup on top and eat hot.

Gourmet touch: *Spoon whipped cream and strawberry jam on top of hot French toast.*
Sensational: *Spoon hot Apple Delight (recipe follows) on hot French Toast, top with vanilla ice cream.*

Apple Delight   

Prep: 5 minutes. Cook: 8-10 minutes. 2 large servings.

Use peeled or unpeeled apples as desired. Delicious as is, hot or cold. Or eat with vanilla ice cream, plain yogurt or cottage cheese. Or spoon some over hot French Toast (recipe above). Or use as a filler for crêpes (recipe on next page).

2 tsp	Cornstarch	10 mL
1/3 cup	Orange juice	75 mL
1/4 tsp	Cinnamon	1 mL
4	Large apples, diced	4

In large microwavable bowl, whisk cornstarch with orange juice and cinnamon until dissolved. Add apples and stir to coat. Cover and microwave at 100% (full power) for 5 minutes. Stir and microwave for 3-5 minutes until tender but not mushy; total cooking time depends on the size and type of apples. (Or cook on stovetop in saucepan, over low heat, until tender; do not overcook.)

Crêpes

Total time: 15 minutes. Makes 8 large crêpes.

Crêpes are very thin, large French pancakes, versatile plain wrappers for both sweet and savory things. Fill some with jam or syrup, or whipped cream and berries, or banana and ice cream. Eat others with canned pears, vanilla ice cream and chocolate syrup. Top some with stir-fried vegetables or ratatouille (page 80) and/or grated cheese and roll them up (heat to melt the cheese). Or make Béchamel sauce (page 92), add sautéed mushrooms or asparagus and grated cheese for a gourmet wrap. Sprinkle some crêpes with sugar while still hot, roll up and keep covered in refrigerator; the sugar melts and tomorrow morning you'll have a tasty breakfast or sweet snack.

3	Large eggs	3
3/4 cup	All-purpose flour	180 mL
1-1/2 cups	Milk	375 mL
	Butter	

In bowl, whisk eggs and flour. Add a little milk and whisk, then add remaining milk and whisk until smooth. Heat nonstick frying pan over medium high heat for 3 minutes. Add a small lump of butter and spread it around until it sizzles. Pour about 1/3 cup (75 mL) of batter into hot frying pan and quickly rotate it to thinly cover bottom (a clean milk carton makes a perfect pitcher for crêpe batter, or use a measuring cup). Cook until light brown underneath. Slip spatula under the crêpe to loosen it, flip it over and brown the other side. Lift it onto a large plate. Stir the batter and make remaining crêpes. (Add a little butter if needed. Additional butter may not be needed for remaining crêpes if the pan is hot enough and crêpe well cooked before flipping it over.)

Orange Ginger Sauce

Total time: 8 minutes.

Delicious, no-fat, sweet sauce for crêpes, pancakes, and vanilla ice cream. Spread cold leftovers on your morning toast.

1 cup	Orange juice	250 mL
1/3 cup	Sugar	75 mL
1 tbsp	Cornstarch	15 mL
1 tbsp	Grated fresh gingerroot	15 mL

In small saucepan on stovetop, stir together all ingredients with wire whisk. Bring to a boil over high heat, stirring constantly. Reduce heat to low and simmer, uncovered, for 5 minutes. Whisk until smooth. Eat warm or cold.

PANCAKES

Total time: 20 minutes. Makes 8 medium or 16 small pancakes.

Freeze leftover pancakes, separated with waxed paper, in self-sealing plastic bags. Defrost in microwave.

1 cup	**All-purpose flour**	**250 mL**
1 tbsp	**Sugar**	**15 mL**
1 tsp	**Baking powder**	**5 mL**
1	**Large egg**	**1**
1 cup	**Milk**	**250 mL**
2 tbsp	**Vegetable oil**	**30 mL**

In medium bowl, mix flour with sugar and baking powder. Make a well in the center of dry ingredients and add egg, milk and oil. Stir with wire whisk until batter is smooth. Heat nonstick frying pan over high heat for 3 minutes. Reduce heat to medium high and grease if desired. Drop the batter in pan by large spoonfuls. Cook until golden brown underneath, flip over and cook the other side. Eat hot or cold with jam or syrup.

Note: A clean milk carton makes a perfect pitcher for pancake batter. To make multigrain pancakes, use equal quantities of whole-wheat flour, buckwheat flour and cornmeal instead of all-purpose flour. See Orange Ginger Sauce on previous page.

BAKED PANCAKE

Prep: 5 minutes. Bake: 25 minutes. 4 generous servings.

This is how they make a delicious pancake in Finland for a soul-satisfying late-night snack or Sunday breakfast. Make hot chocolate or a pot of tea to go with your pancake; cold milk is good too. Spread some jam on cold leftover pancake for a tasty and fast breakfast.

2	**Large eggs**	**2**
3 tbsp	**Sugar**	**45 mL**
Pinch	**Salt**	**Pinch**
3/4 cup	**All-purpose flour**	**180 mL**
1-1/2 cups	**Milk**	**375 mL**

Preheat oven to 425°F (220°C). Grease 4 round, disposable aluminum pie plates (perfect for this recipe since they bake the bottom golden crisp; wash and use repeatedly), or one large baking sheet. In large bowl, stir together eggs, sugar, salt and flour with wire whisk for 2 minutes. Whisk in the milk until smooth. Pour the batter in prepared pie plates or baking sheet. Bake for 25 minutes until golden brown. Cut into wedges or squares and eat warm or cold with sugar, maple syrup or jam.

Fried Bananas

Total time: 8 minutes.

Satisfy your sweet tooth & get rid of those old bananas. For special occasions, make plenty, and on each plate, add a drizzle of real maple syrup and perhaps a splash of rum or cognac plus a dollop of vanilla ice cream.

Butter
Ripe bananas
Brown sugar
(Canned pineapple slices or tidbits, peach halves)

Melt a lump of butter in frying pan at medium high. Peel bananas, cut in half, then slit each piece in half lengthwise. Put banana slices in hot frying pan over sizzling butter, sprinkle generously with brown sugar. Fry both sides at medium high until golden. The sugar will melt and caramelize. Do not burn. Eat with vanilla ice cream and sprinkle some instant chocolate on top. (For a delicious variation, fry canned pineapple and peach halves along with bananas.)

Frozen Sweet Stuff

- **Bananas:** When your bananas threaten to turn black, freeze them. Peel and smash with fork, put on a plate, make airtight cover with plastic wrap and freeze for a few hours until solid; eat the yummy frozen bananas with a spoon for a sweet snack. (Or freeze unpeeled bananas; peel with sharp knife and use for Fried Bananas; see recipe on this page. Or freeze mashed bananas in a plastic bag and use later for Banana Muffins, see recipe on page 101.)

- **Grapes:** Red seedless grapes are best for this treat since they are very sweet. Remove grapes from stems, rinse & dry, freeze in a bowl overnight. Eat frozen.

- **Jell-O:** Frozen gelatin makes a sweet, icy treat and also soothes a sore throat. Make gelatin as shown on the package. Put it in a small bowl and freeze for 4 hours until solid; eat with spoon. Or freeze it in an ice-cube tray, pry cubes out and store in a plastic bag in the freezer so the surface won't dry out.

- **Frozen fruit brochettes:** Push a bamboo skewer through your choice of fruits (pineapple cubes, strawberries, grapes, banana cubes, honeydew and cantaloupe cubes, watermelon chunks). Put brochettes into a plastic bag, seal tightly and freeze. Great for hot days. Watermelon is particularly delicious even on its own when frozen. Just before devouring your frozen fruit, drizzle with some bottled chocolate shell topping, the kind that hardens in seconds and cracks when you eat it.

Apple Oatmeal Crisp For Two

Prep: 4 minutes. Bake: 5 minutes in microwave, or 25 minutes in regular oven. 2 servings.

Delicious as is or top with vanilla ice cream.

2	Apples, peeled and cut bite-size	2
2 tbsp	Brown sugar	30 mL
Dash	Ground cinnamon	Dash
2 tbsp each	All-purpose flour and butter	30 mL each
1/2 cup	Rolled oats	125 mL

Spread apples in microwavable dish, sprinkle with sugar and cinnamon. Spread flour on top, add butter cut in small pieces, top with oats. Microwave at 100% (full power) for 5 minutes, stir. Or bake in ovenproof casserole at 375°F (190°C) for 25 minutes until apples are very tender and brown sugar melts.

Light and crispy variation: Omit flour and butter.

Coconut Chews

Prep: 15 minutes. Bake: 45 minutes. Makes 25 squares.

1 cup	Rolled oats	250 mL
1 cup	Shredded coconut	250 mL
1 cup	Dates, cut into small pieces with sharp knife or scissors	250 mL
4 tbsp	Butter, melted	60 mL
1/2 cup	Liquid honey, heated*	125 mL
2	Large eggs	2

**Heating honey makes it easy to mix well with dry ingredients.*

Preheat oven to 325°F (160°C). Line a cake pan (9" or 23 cm square) with waxed paper, set aside. In bowl, mix all ingredients until well blended. Spread the mixture into prepared cake pan (dip spoon in water and press the mixture flat). Bake for 45 minutes. Cool, lift it out of the pan, discard the waxed paper and cut into small squares.

Make a pitcher of refreshing iced tea or a nice hot mug of coffee bliss (see next page).

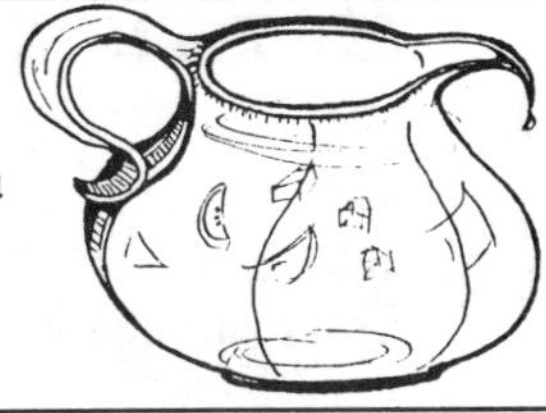

SWEET STUFF

Coffee Bliss

Fill a nice big mug with hot, strong coffee. Do not add any sugar. Scoop a ball of vanilla ice cream on top and let it begin to melt for just a few seconds. Then sip and enjoy this exquisite gourmet treat. Impress other coffee aficionados.

Café Au Lait

Fill a big mug with hot milk, add a heaping teaspoon of instant coffee granules and sugar to taste. A delicious treat for coffee lovers.

Iced Coffee Soda

Refrigerate leftover coffee. Drop a scoop of vanilla ice cream into a tall glass, fill the glass with cold coffee and cream soda. (Sweeten with sugar if desired.)

Iced Tea

In pitcher, put 3 tea bags and 1/2 cup (125 mL) of sugar. Pour 4 cups (1 L) of boiling water on top. Stir gently until sugar is dissolved. Let sit for 5 minutes on countertop, then remove tea bags. Add 4 cups (1 L) of cold water, stir and chill for 4 hours. If you're in a rush, pour 4 cups (1 L) of boiling water over tea bags and sugar, stir, then fill the pitcher with ice cubes instead of cold water.

Float

Drop a scoop of vanilla ice cream into a tall glass, fill with root beer. For a Snow Float, use a scoop of vanilla ice cream and fill the glass with cream soda.

Mom's Hot Honey-Lemon Drink

Drop a generous dollop of honey and a spoonful of fresh or bottled lemon juice into a nice big mug. Fill with hot water and stir to mix. It soothes your cold and winter chills. Stir with a cinnamon stick.

Hot Juice

Hot juice is a great comforter to sip on a cold, late night. Heat a mugful of juice to almost the boiling point (in microwave or on stovetop). Especially good are cranberry, cranberry-blueberry, apple, lingonberry and black currant juices. (Lingonberry and black currant juices are available as a concentrate in stores specializing in European imports.)

SHAKES & SMOOTHIES

If you have a blender, you can make delicious shakes and smoothies in seconds. The quantities and ingredients are flexible so follow your taste. Always leave enough room for the froth so it won't spill all over the place when you turn the blender on. Put all the ingredients into the blender. Cover and blend on high speed for 20 seconds until smooth. For a variation, try soy milk instead of regular milk.

Each recipe makes 1-2 large servings. Serve shakes and smoothies immediately.

ICED COFFEE MILKSHAKE
1 cup (250 mL) milk, 1 tbsp (15 mL) instant coffee powder, 1 tbsp (15 mL) sugar, three ice cubes.

BANANA MILKSHAKE
1/2 cup (125 mL) vanilla ice cream, 1 cup (250 mL) milk, one banana, three ice cubes. (A splash of vanilla extract.)

CHOCOLATE SHAKE
1/2 cup (125 mL) chocolate ice cream, 1 cup (250 mL) milk, three ice cubes.

PEACHY PASSION
1 cup (250 mL) peaches & juice, 1 cup (250 mL) apple juice, three ice cubes.

CRANBERRY CRUSH
1 cup (250 mL) cranberry cocktail, 1 cup (250 mL) orange juice, one ripe banana, three ice cubes.

THICK TROPICAL SHAKE
1/2 cup (125 mL) crushed pineapple, one ripe banana, 1 cup (250 mL) plain yogurt, 3 tbsp (45 mL) coconut flakes, three ice cubes.

ORANGE SMOOTHIE
1 cup (250 mL) cold orange juice, one ripe banana, three ice cubes (& a pinch of grated gingerroot).
Deluxe version: Add flesh from 1/2 ripe mango and/or several fresh or frozen strawberries, and blend until smooth.

Ricebag Heatpad

This "bonus recipe" is not to eat but it comforts your aches and colds and warms away the chills.

You know those nice grain-filled heatpads they sell in stores? You can make a "student's version" in a jiffy. Put six cups (1.5 L) of uncooked rice into a small cotton pillowcase, close with a rubberband or stitch tightly shut (rice should move around freely). Microwave for 3 minutes whenever you need a warm touch. Drape the hot bag around your shoulders, back or under your feet, and take your new pal to bed with you. (Use repeatedly for this purpose only; do not reuse that same rice for cooking.)

INDEX

☑ **Mark your favorite recipes so you'll find them fast next time.**

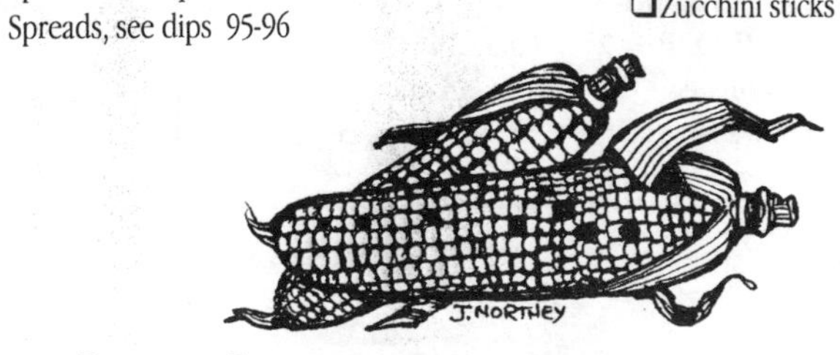
J. NORTHEY

Start a miniature garden on your sunny windowsill to grow fresh herbs like parsley, mint, and basil.

Do you have an original recipe to share, comments or questions? I would love to hear from you. Write to:

Leila Peltosaari
c/o TIKKA BOOKS
P. O. Box 242, Chambly
Quebec J3L 4B3 Canada
email: lpeltosaari@tikkabooks.qc.ca
web-site: tikkabooks.qc.ca

ISBN 1-896106-01-3
Spiral binding, 123 pages

COLLEGE CUISINE

EASY, CHEAP, FAST, NUTRITIOUS RECIPES FOR STUDENTS

BY LEILA PELTOSAARI
ILLUSTRATED BY JULIE NORTHEY

ALL STUDENTS EAT. SMART STUDENTS COOK.

A student's first cookbook and kitchen companion. Makes a great gift. Let this manual guide you to culinary independence.

- **GETTING STARTED.** *Equipment & staples, cooking terms, imperial/metric conversion, substitutions, shopping, safety, cleaning tips, fixing mistakes.*
- **RESCUE PERISHABLES.** *Recipes for perishables before they go bad, shelf life.*
- **BREAKFASTS, LUNCHES TO GO, SANDWICHES.**
- **BASICS.** *Learning to cook eggs, beans, pasta, potatoes & rice.*
- **MINUTE MEALS, MIDNIGHT SNACKS, MICROWAVE MIRACLES.**
- **SOUPS, SALADS AND SALAD DRESSINGS.**
- **MEAT, CHICKEN, FISH & VEGETARIAN RECIPES.**
- **CROWD PLEASERS.**
- **BAKING BREADS, MUFFINS, CAKES AND COOKIES.**
- **SWEET STUFF & BEVERAGES, MILKSHAKES & SMOOTHIES.**

Over 150 recipes

ORDER FORM **TIKKA BOOKS**

PO Box 242,
Chambly Quebec J3L 4B3 Canada
Tel. (450) 658-6205, fax (450) 658-3514
email: lpeltosaari@tikkabooks.qc.ca

- ❑ Please send me ——— copies of ***College Cuisine***. Canada: $12.95 (add $3 for shipping/tax; total Can$15.95). USA: $9.95 (add $3 for shipping; total US$12.95).
- ❑ Please send me your special offer. I buy five copies and the sixth copy is free of charge. Total Can$79.75 (US$64.75).

NAME ______________________ DATE __________

ADDRESS ______________________ TEL.# __________

CITY __________ PROVINCE OR STATE __________ POSTAL CODE OR ZIP __________

❑ CHEQUE OR MONEY ORDER ENCLOSED FOR $ __________

❑ VISA/MASTERCARD# __________

EXP.DATE __________ SIGNATURE __________

ORDER FORM **TIKKA BOOKS**

PO Box 242,
Chambly Quebec J3L 4B3 Canada
Tel. (450) 658-6205, fax (450) 658-3514
email: lpeltosaari@tikkabooks.qc.ca

- ❑ Please send me ——— copies of ***College Cuisine***. Canada: $12.95 (add $3 for shipping/tax; total Can$15.95). USA: $9.95 (add $3 for shipping; total US$12.95).
- ❑ Please send me your special offer. I buy five copies and the sixth copy is free of charge. Total Can$79.75 (US$64.75).

NAME ______________________ DATE __________

ADDRESS ______________________ TEL.# __________

CITY __________ PROVINCE OR STATE __________ POSTAL CODE OR ZIP __________

❑ CHEQUE OR MONEY ORDER ENCLOSED FOR $ __________

❑ VISA/MASTERCARD# __________

EXP.DATE __________ SIGNATURE __________